A Quick Guide to the Internet

Julia Case Bradley
Mt. San Antonio College

INTEGRATED MEDIA GROUP

I(T)P™ An International Thomson Publishing Company

Belmont • Albany • Bonn • Boston • Cincinnati • Detroit • London • Madrid • Melbourne
Mexico City • New York • Paris • San Francisco • Singapore • Tokyo • Toronto • Washington

Multimedia Editor: Kathy Shields
Assistant Editor: Tamara Huggins
Production Services Coordinator: Gary Mcdonald
Production: Linda Mumbauer
Designer: Linda Mumbauer
Print Buyer: Karen Hunt
Copy Editor: Margaret Moore
Cover: Stephen Rapley
Compositor: Julia Case Bradley
Printer: Malloy Lithographing

Printed in the United States of America
1 2 3 4 5 6 7 8 9 10—01 00 99 98 97 96 95

For more information, contact Wadsworth Publishing Company:

Wadsworth Publishing Company
10 Davis Drive
Belmont, California 94002, USA

International Thomson Publishing Europe
Berkshire House 168-173
High Holborn
London, WC1V 7AA, England

Thomas Nelson Australia
102 Dodds Street
South Melbourne 3205
Victoria, Australia

Nelson Canada
1120 Birchmount Road
Scarborough, Ontario
Canada M1K 5G4

International Thomson Editores
Campos Eliseos 385, Piso 7
Col. Polanco
11560 México D.F. México

International Thomson Publishing GmbH
Königswinterer Strasse 418
53227 Bonn, Germany

International Thomson Publishing Asia
221 Henderson Road
#05-10 Henderson Building
Singapore 0315

International Thomson Publishing Japan
Hirakawacho Kyowa Building, 3F
2-2-1 Hirakawacho
Chiyoda-ku, Tokyo 102, Japan

We would like to thank the following reviewers: Susan Michael, University of Kentucky; George Sellman, Adams State College; and David Stephan, Baruch College–CUNY.

ISBN 0-534-26076-4

Contents

1   THE INTERNET — AN OVERVIEW **1**
   Welcome to the Internet 1
   What Is the Internet? 1
   What Can You Do on the Internet? 4
   Names, Addresses, and Domains 6
   Netiquette 8

2   COMMUNICATING WITH EMAIL **9**
   Who Can You Talk To? 9
   Mail Reader Software 9
   Creating and Sending Messages 10
   Reading Your Messages 11
   Replying to Messages 12
   Mail Etiquette 13
   Try This 13
   Mail Problems 14
   Mail Command Reference 15

3   DISCUSSING INTERESTS IN USENET NEWSGROUPS ___ **17**
   What Is the Usenet? 17
   The Organization of Usenet Newsgroups 18
   News Reader Software 19

   Reading Newsgroup Postings 19
   Responding to Newsgroup Posting 20
   Newsgroup Frequently Asked Questions
   (FAQ) Files 20
   Usenet Etiquette 20
   Abbreviations 21
   Try This 21
   Usenet Problems 22
   Usenet Command Reference 23

4   RECEIVING INFORMATION FROM MAILING LISTS ____ **25**
   Using Mailing Lists 25
   Finding Mailing Lists 26
   Subscribing to Mailing Lists 26
   Responding to Mailing List Postings 27
   Unsubscribing from Mailing Lists 27
   Requesting More Information 28
   Try this 28
   Mailing List Problems 29
   Mailing List Command Reference 30

5   TELNETTING TO OTHER COMPUTER SITES _____ **31**
   Logging On to Other Computer Sites 31
   Understanding Terminal Babel 32
   Issuing Telnet Commands 32

Finding Sites to Telnet To 34
Try This 34
Telnet Problems 35
Telnet Command Reference 37

6   TRANSFERRING FILES USING FTP _____ **39**
Using Ftp to Retrieve Files from
Other Computers 39
Using Anonymous Ftp 40
Searching the Directories for the
Files You Want 41
Transferring Files 42
Signing Off 46
Try This 46
Ftp Problems 47
Ftp Command Reference 48

7   LOCATING FILES USING ARCHIE _____ **51**
Archie's Archives 51
Using a Local Archie Client Program 51
Telnetting to a Remote Archie 52
Contacting Archie by Email 55
Try This 56

Archie Problems 56
Archie Command Reference 57

8   LOCATING INFORMATION USING GOPHER _____ **59**
Sending Gopher to Find Information 59
Using a Local Gopher Client Program 60
Telnetting to a Remote Gopher 62
Try This 63
Gopher Problems 64
Gopher Command Reference 65

9   GETTING HELP FROM VERONICA _____ **67**
Veronica's Archives 67
Beginning Your Search 68
Try This 71
Veronica Problems 71
Veronica Command Reference.................... 72

10 NAVIGATING THE WORLD WIDE WEB (WWW) ____ **73**
Jumping Around the Net Using Hypertext 73
Addressing Net Resources by URL 74
Browser Programs 74
Browsing with a Text Mode Program 75

Browsing with a Graphical Program 76
Try This 76
WWW Browser Problems 78
WWW Line-Mode Browser
Command Reference 79
Browsing with Mosaic 80

**11 SEARCHING DATABASES WITH
WIDE AREA INFORMATION SERVERS (WAIS) _____ 81**
Finding Indexed Data 81
Using a Local WAIS Client Program 82
Telnetting to a Remote WAIS Client Site 82
Gophering to a WAIS Search 82
Performing a WAIS Search 82
Try This 84
WAIS Problems 84
WAIS Commands 84

12 USING INTERNET TOOLS _____ 85
The UNIX Heritage 85
Finger 85
Ping 86
Whois 87

13 CHATTING, TALKING AND PLAYING GAMES _____ 89
Having Fun on the Net...................................... 89
Using Talk 89
Chatting with IRC.. 90
Try This 92
IRC Command Reference 93
Playing Games 94

**14 DOWNLOADING, DECOMPRESSING, AND
DECODING FILES _____ 95**
Downloading Files 95
Xmodem.. 95
Zmodem 96
Kermit 96
Decompressing and Decoding Files 97
Including a Binary File in an Email Message 99

GLOSSARY _____ 101

INDEX _____ 107

THE INTERNET — AN OVERVIEW

Welcome to the Internet

What Is the Internet?

What Can You Do on the Internet?

Names, Addresses, and Domains

Netiquette

Welcome to the Internet

Would you like to send messages to a friend half-way around the globe? You can do that, as well as discuss your favorite hobby with other enthusiasts, research information in one of the varied databases or libraries, keep up with breaking news stories, check sports schedules and outcomes, discuss interests or problems with others, participate in one of the huge Multiuser Dungeon (MUD) games, locate and download movie reviews, graphics, sounds, and even whole books.

The Internet is the place. All these things, and *lots* more, are going on 24 hours a day, over the entire earth. You can ask a question on the net, and receive an answer in a few minutes from Zaire, or France, or Australia, or Germany, or India, or Canada, or . . .

What Is the Internet?

Although many people like to think of the Internet as one huge global network, that simply isn't true. The Internet is a collection of *many* networks, some very large, and some as small as a single computer. When you start exploring the Internet, you will find computer systems run by colleges and universities, corporations, organizations, the US government (and many other governments), and online service providers, such as Delphi, America Online, and CompuServe.

Since the Internet is actually many *independent* networks connected together, there is no central authority or official rules. (Notice the emphasis on *independent*.) Each site is in charge of its own system and can make its own rules. At any time, a site may elect to add or delete some services. If you are unhappy with the rules at any site, you can appeal to the site administrator; but you cannot appeal to a "higher authority"—because there is none.

A good way to think about the Internet is like many cities and towns, connected by highways. You can use the highways to travel from town to town. Some towns have lots of places to explore; and in some cities, you could spend years and never find all of the hidden "goodies." If you think of the Internet in this way, many of its concepts will make sense:

- Each site is "governed" by the local authorities.
- It takes some exploring on your own to locate things of interest to you.
- There is more than one path ("road") to get from one location to another.

- The individuals in one location may have different ways of doing things than in another location (like yours). These things may include their values, their language, their customs, their rules (or lack of rules).
- You will find many varied interest groups. Just as you choose your own friends in real life, you can choose your online friends. You may also find some souls with which you would rather not associate.
- Think of each "city" as a foreign place. They will certainly *feel* foreign to you at first. There are many different types of computer systems, with many different command languages. This means that to communicate with some of these systems, you may need to learn some of their language (such as UNIX commands).

The Roots of the Net

The Internet began as an experiment in the 1960s by the US Defense Department's Advanced Research Projects Agency (ARPA). The scientists working on the projects were looking for a way to use computers for communicating with each other. And the Defense Department wanted to create a network that could keep functioning, even if individual sites could no longer operate, in the event of a nuclear war.

To build this flexible network, ARPA adopted a plan where all data traveling on the network is broken into "packets." Each packet of information holds a destination address and time stamp. The packets can move on the network in a manner called "store and forward." Each computer picks out the packets addressed for that site, and passes the rest on to another site. The individual packets for one document can take different paths, until they arrive at the correct computer. At their destination, the packets are reassembled into the correct order. This method, called TCP/IP (Transmission Control Protocol/Internet Protocol) is still in use today, and is the basis for the worldwide network of networks called the Internet.

As an analogy, think of the Internet as the US Postal Service. Say you are in New York, and you want to send a paperback book to your friend in San Francisco. However, your envelopes hold only 100 pages, and the book is 500 pages long. So you divide the book into five chunks, place each piece into a separate envelope, number the envelopes in order, address and send them. The packages don't go directly to San Francisco, but instead, they are sent to your local Post Office. From there, the packages likely move to a regional Post Office, and then on to the next location (that's store-and-forward). If one of the links in the chain had a problem—say a flood wiped out the regional center—no problem; the packages would just take an alternate route. And it's possible that the five packages could take different routes to their final destination, and that package 5 might arrive before package 1. When your friend receives all five packages, she can assemble them in order and have the complete book.

As a side note: The world saw how well the TCP/IP network concept can work during the war with Iraq, when it was not possible to bring down the Iraqi communication network.

The Growth of the Net
The original network, called ARPAnet, grew to include scientists and researchers from government, military, and universities. Then students and faculty began experimenting with networking. Many separate networks were created, such as UUCP (UNIX-to-UNIX CoPy) and bitnet (because it's time network). In the 80's, the National Science Foundation (NSF) computer

became the main "backbone" of the net, and the network became known as the Internet (internetworking networks). Through the 80's and into the 90's, more and more universities, organizations, and companies have connected to this network.

The growth rate of the Internet during the 90's has become exponential. Although nobody knows exactly how many users have access to the net, estimates in early 1994 range from 20 million to 30 million. And the number of users is increasing by millions each month.

Clients and Servers, Working Together

The mechanics of the net can be divided into two parts—service providers and service users. The providers, called *servers,* supply services and information, such as databases, files, indexes to stored documents, messages, graphics, and sound. The users of the information are called *clients.* Both servers and clients are software—the computer programs that do the work. However, the computer (hardware) that holds the server program and its information may also be referred to as the server.

Client software and server software work together to supply the information you request. A server usually resides on a large computer somewhere; client programs reside either on your own computer or on the main computer for your local network. The client programs request services of the server programs. Then, when the requested information arrives, the client programs take care of the local processing, such as formatting the screen, allowing you to save, delete, catalog, reply, and so on. For example, you will learn to use gopher to locate stored resources. Your local computer or network must have installed a gopher client program. The local gopher client will query a remote gopher server, located on another computer on the net. The gopher server will send the requested information, which your local gopher client will present on your screen.

What Can You Do on the Internet?

The list of services available on the net keeps growing. In order to be an informed user, you will want to know about the following topics. Each of these subjects is covered in more depth in later chapters of this guide.

- **Email**
  Electronic mail, or email, is one of the greatest features of the net. You can send a message to someone at your local site, or any of the

approximately 30 million users, anywhere in the world. Email is usually the first Internet service a person learns to use; and many people are satisfied to stop there and *only* use email.

- **Usenet Newsgroups and Mailing Lists**
Usenet newsgroups are the means to carry on discussions with other people who share your interests. You can follow discussions on many topics, and add your own opinions if you choose. Newsgroups are similar to groups on other systems called *forums*, *BBSs* (bulletin board systems), or *SIGs* (special interest groups). However, don't call newsgroups by any of those other names, unless you want to sound like an uninitiated "newbie."

Mailing lists are similar to newsgroups, but the discussion messages are mailed directly to your electronic mailbox. The messages come to you, rather than you going to the newsgroup.

- **Telnet**
The feature that allows you to login to remote computers is called *telnet*. You can telnet to any computer on the net for which you have an account. In addition, many computers allow you to login as a guest to use some of its programs. You can use telnet to login to supercomputers and government computers, your home computer when traveling, or any one of hundreds of computers that allow external logins.

- **Ftp and Archie**
Ftp (file transfer protocol) is the method you will use to transfer files from a remote computer to your local host. But how can you find where the files are? If you are looking for a program, archie can help you find it. You can use an archie server to search remote sites, all over the world. After archie locates the program you're looking for, you can use ftp to transfer it.

- **Gopher and Veronica**
Gopher and veronica are two more ways to search for information on the net. Gopher can "tunnel" around the net, find files that you request, and present its results in menu form. Veronica searches a master index that holds topic titles from all over the net, and can quickly locate files.

- **WWW and Mosaic**
  One of the newest features of the Internet is WWW (World Wide Web). The WWW project is the most "user friendly" approach to using the Internet. You can search for information using "hyper" links, which allow you to select new topics from words or buttons appearing on the screen, and jump to the requested spot. The WWW project is working to create hypertext pages at locations all over the net, so that any available information can be found with a WWW client program.

  There are several WWW client programs available. The leading program, called Mosaic, presents hypertext pages in a graphical user interface, and is extremely easy to learn. There is a version of Mosaic for the Macintosh, one for Windows, and one for X-Windows. Mosaic was developed by the National Center for Supercomputing Applications (NCSA), and is distributed free.

- **WAIS**
  WAIS (Wide Area Information Servers) are a relatively new feature of the Internet. WAIS servers can search indexes of databases, all over the net for *content* rather than just for titles (like veronica and archie searches).

- **IRC and Talk**
  Would you like to converse with other people over the net, without waiting for email or newsgroup messages to be read? You can use IRC (Internet Relay Chat) and Talk to carry on conversations in "real time" (happening at the current moment). IRC is similar to CB radio channels, where many people can be conversing on one channel. With Talk, you carry on an electronic conversation with one person, one-on-one.

Names, Addresses, and Domains
Every host computer attached to the net has an address assigned to it. And every person using the net has an address which refers to their host address.

The actual address assigned to each host computer is a long number. But fortunately, each computer also has a name. Most of the time, you won't care about the numbers, but just call computers by name. However, you should know the number of your own host—the computer that you use, which is attached to the Internet. You probably should also know the number for another computer nearby, in case of problems. (On occasion, the program that matches computer names to numbers gets fouled up. In this case, you may need to know the computer's numeric address.)

Computer addresses are assigned as four groups of numbers, separated by periods—called a "dotted quad." For example, the numeric address of my host computer is 140.144.204.50. But, for practically all purposes, you can refer to *ibm.mtsac.edu* and get the same computer.

Host computer names are assigned according to a naming convention. Within the United States, the suffix (ending) of the name usually indicates the type of organization. For computers in other parts of the world, the suffix usually indicates the country.

US host domain suffixes:

com	Commercial organizations
edu	Educational institutions
gov	Government organizations and departments
int	International organizations, such as NATO
mil	Military sites
net	Networking organizations
org	Miscellaneous organizations that don't fit any other classification, such as professional societies

Organizations in countries other than the United States generally use a two-character suffix that indicates the country. (Some organizations in the US also use the "us" suffix.) Here are a few of the possibilities:

au	Australia
ca	Canada
fr	France
de	Germany
il	Israel
jp	Japan
se	Sweden
ch	Switzerland
us	United States

Netiquette

Have you ever been in a strange location and said or done something that was totally out of place? It's easy to do, until you learn the local customs.

Think of the Internet as a foreign society, with its own traditions. The best approach is to listen and watch awhile, and remember not to judge others by your own local norms.

Some words of advice for Internet "newbies":

- Be kind and considerate of others. And don't be surprised to find a few people who are not.
- Before you ask a question of a newsgroup, find and read their FAQ (Frequently Asked Questions) file. You can find the FAQ file in the newsgroup itself; or in the group: `news.answers`, which serves as a repository for FAQs from many groups.
- Type in lowercase characters, with proper capitalization. PEOPLE WHO TYPE IN ALL CAPITALS ARE SAID TO BE SHOUTING. It is actually much easier to read lowercase.
- Don't overdo the exclamations!!!! Or any other <<<<$%#@&*>>>> symbols.

- If you wish to add a signature, keep it short. A signature is a file that is appended to the end of your postings and email messages. As you explore newsgroups, you will likely find some entertaining signatures. Keep yours to no more than four lines, out of courtesy to others.
- When accessing another computer system by telnet or ftp, you are a guest. Be considerate. Plan to use other systems during their slow time. Many system administrators limit telnet or ftp access to a certain number of connections, or to a given time period (typically 6pm—6am, *their* local time).

Are you ready? Let's start the fun.

Who Can You Talk To?

Who do you want to talk to? Assuming that your host computer has electronic mail (email) capability, you can send and receive messages to anyone on your local system, or anyone connected to the Internet, anywhere in the world. You can even send email messages to many others; many computer systems have a mail gateway attached to the Internet, even if they don't have a full Internet connection.

To send email, you need mail reader software and the electronic address of someone. The way most systems are set up, you can send messages to anyone on your local system using only his login ID as the address. For a person elsewhere on the net, you will need his entire address. For example, anyone on my local system can send me mail addressed to `jbradley`. But someone on another computer system would need to address it to `jbradley@ibm.mtsac.edu`. The segment of the address following the "at sign" (@) is needed to direct the mail to the correct host computer.

Mail Reader Software

There are many different mail reader programs available. What that means is that there are lots of different ways to accomplish the same set of tasks. You

---

COMMUNICATING WITH EMAIL

Who Can You Talk To?

Mail Reader Software

Creating and Sending Messages

Reading Your Messages

Replying to Messages

Mail Etiquette

Try This

Mail Problems

Mail Command Reference

---

will need to be able to read your messages, respond to messages, create and send new messages, and save or delete both incoming and outgoing messages. It is also nice to be able to forward messages, send a message to a list of names, send complimentary copies, request acknowledgment of a message, and keep an address book of names and email addresses.

All mail reader programs have the basic set of commands; some also have extra "bells and whistles." For example, your mail program may allow you to file messages in folders by topic or by user, or retrieve messages after they have been sent.

Since each mail reader program uses different commands, it's not likely that yours will be covered here. Instead, make a note of your commands on the Mail Command Reference page (see page 15). Since the most-used mail program is the UNIX Mail program, those commands will be given here. (Note that it is "most-used," not "most-popular." With a little luck, you may be using a great graphical program, where you can click on icons to make things happen.)

Creating and Sending Messages
Your first task is to launch your mail program and begin

a new message. Although the command will vary, depending on your computer system and your mail reader software, the usual method is to type the name of the program, followed by the email address of the person to whom you are writing. Example:

To start mail on a UNIX system, and begin a new message, type:
Mail *username@useraddress*
(of course, fill in actual username and useraddress.)

Enter the Subject Header
When you begin a new message, usually you will be prompted to enter the subject of your message. Type a subject and press Enter. Note that there is an art to writing good subject headers. If you are writing to a person who receives lots of mail, she will appreciate a well-written subject header. For example,

This is much better .... than this.

Where to find history database?	I need help!
FAQ for movie database?	Where can I find information?
How to delete mail message?	HELP!!!!! (avoid all caps and excess punctuation)

Type Your Message

After entering the address and subject, you can type the text of your message. Most mail programs do not automatically wrap text, so you must press Enter after every 60 or 70 characters. (Later, when you are reading messages and news postings, you will find that some people don't worry about the ends of lines. It looks sloppy.)

When you have finished your message, *proofread it*. If your mail program has a spell checker, use it. *Then*, send it. How you end (and send) your message varies. With UNIX Mail, type a period as the first character of the line and press Enter. UNIX Mail will prompt you for a Cc: (complimentary copy); press Enter and the message is sent.

Your mail program will have a command for sending a message—investigate. For example, for my mail program, I must press F5 to send off the completed message. Read your screen, check the Help file, read the manual, or ask someone. Then, write the command on the Mail Command Reference page (page 15).

HELP   You can cancel a message any time before sending it: In UNIX Mail, press Ctrl+c twice. In the program I use, F12 cancels. Check your program documentation.

Send a Test Message

Send a test message to yourself; it's easy. For the address of the recipient, just type your own email address. Or, send one to a friend.

Reading Your Messages

You will need to learn to read your incoming mail, as well as file it, delete it, and respond to it.

The procedure for reading your mail depends on the mail reader program you are using. Some mail programs automatically display your in-basket, or your first message, when you launch the program. For others, you must request your incoming mail. If you are lucky enough to be using a mail program with a graphical interface, you may have an icon that indicates mail waiting. Depending on your system, you may request incoming messages by making a menu choice, clicking an icon, pressing a function key, or typing a command.

Whatever mail program you are using, you will be able to view a list of your incoming messages. Generally the messages are listed, one per line, showing the ID of the sender, the date and time sent, and the subject header. Most mail programs also have an indicator to tell you which messages are new, which you have read, and which ones were there but unread on your last visit.

You can choose to read any (or all) of your messages. You can also reply to a message, save it, and/or delete it.

Replying to Messages

When you reply to messages, it's best to refresh the memory of the person who sent the original message. I get *lots* of mail and am sometimes puzzled by a brief reply that just says "Thanks" or "That sounds good to me."

A common practice on the net is to repeat (or echo) the relevant part of the original message, then type your reply. That may sound like a lot of trouble, but it's usually quite easy. Most mail programs will echo the message—either automatically or by request—placing a symbol at the beginning of each line to indicate the quote. Your job is to delete the lines that are not relevant to the topic, then type your reply. (*Don't* leave in their entire message—that's a waste.)

For example, here is a message I received (in my dreams):

```
To:        jbradley@ibm.mtsac.edu
Subject:   dinner party Sat. eve.
From:      president@whitehouse.gov
The President of the United States requests the
pleasure of your company at a dinner party Saturday
evening at 8:00. Dress casual.
R.S.V.P
```

And my reply, correctly done:

```
To:        president@whitehouse.gov
Subject:   Re: dinner party Sat. eve.
From:      jbradley@ibm.mtsac.edu
>The President of the United States requests
>the pleasure of your company at a dinner
>party Saturday evening at 8:00. Dress
>casual.
>R.S.V.P.
Sure, I'd be happy to attend.
```

Your mail program will have a command to reply to messages, with or without echoing the original message. Investigate your program, and write the command on the Mail Command Reference page (page 15).

Mail Etiquette

Do:

- Be polite; remember that your recipient is a human being, not a computer. Don't say anything that you wouldn't say to the person's face.
- Type using lowercase. When you use uppercase, PEOPLE THINK YOU'RE SHOUTING.
- Remember that your reader can't see your face or body language, and attempts at humor are often misinterpreted. Use a smiley to indicate that you are joking:

  smiley: :-) or :)
  winking smiley: ;-)
  smiley with glasses: 8-)
  sad face: :-(
  plus many more...

- Keep messages brief and to the point. Rambling text loses the reader's attention, and annoys those who must pay for their online service.
- Remember that your email may not be private. Say only those things that you wouldn't mind seeing posted on the bulletin board. And *never* send your credit card number or password via email.

Don't:

- Send any chain letters. You will make enemies on the net.
- Use excess punctuation marks!!!!!!!!!!!!!!!!

Try This

- Send a test message to yourself.
  Enter your own email address for the recipient. Write a good subject header and a message you'll be glad to receive.
- Wait for the test message, then read it.
  You may need to exit the mail program and re-enter, in order to see your incoming mail. Usually mail for the local site is delivered very quickly.
- Reply to your test message.
  If your mail program provides a way, include your original message in the reply. At the end of the original message, type a response and send it off. It should arrive in your in-basket shortly.
- Read the reply and save it.
- Delete the reply from your in-basket.
- Send a message to the president or another elected official.
  For the president of the United States, address your message to
  president@whitehouse.gov

Or, for the vice-president, write to

`vice-president@whitehouse.gov`

- Send a message to a server at Oregon State University. You will receive a return message with an "uplifting" quote. Address your message to

`almanac@oes.orst.edu`

Leave the subject line blank, and type a one-line message:

`send moral-support`

- Send a message to a friend, with cc (complimentary copy; sometimes called carbon copy) to yourself or another friend.
- Forward a message from your in-basket to a friend.

Mail Problems

If you have problems with email, try these tactics:

- Read the screen, looking for Help. You may be able to look up instructions online.
- Read the manual. Some systems have the manual stored online. Try `man mail` (insert the name of your mail program for "mail").
- Ask someone around you for help.
- Ask your local system administrator for help—by email, telephone, or in person.
- Do not send a question out on the Internet if it concerns your local mail program or system setup. Locate someone at your site who can answer your questions.

Mail Command Reference
Name of your email program _____

Command	UNIX Mail	Your Email Program
Launch email program	mail	
Exit email program	q	
Launch program and begin a new message	mail *userid@useraddress*	
Read a message	Type message number and press Enter	
Save a message	s *msgnumbers filename*	
Delete a message	d *msgnumbers*	
Reply to a message	r *msgnumber*	
Reply to a message, including the text of the original	Reply and type ~f *msgnumber* at the beginning of a line to include the original message	
Send complimentary copy (cc)	Fill in the Cc: prompt when beginning a new message	
Forward a message	Begin a new message and type ~f *msgnumber* at the beginning of a line to include the message to forward	
Cancel a message without sending it	Ctrl+c, Ctrl+c	

overview email newsgroups mailing lists telnet ftp

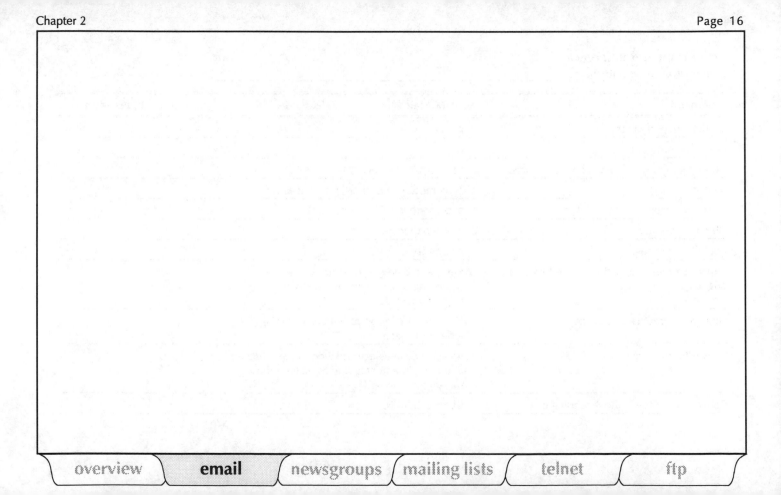

DISCUSSING INTERESTS IN USENET NEWSGROUPS

What Is the Usenet?

The Organization of Usenet Newsgroups

News Reader Software

Reading Newsgroup Postings

Responding to Newsgroup Posting

Newsgroup Frequently Asked Questions (FAQ) Files

Usenet Etiquette

Abbreviations

Try This

Usenet Problems

Usenet Command Reference

What Is the Usenet?

The Usenet (user network) is a giant collection of discussion groups. You can find a group conversing about almost anything, including sports, such as baseball, scuba, rugby, soccer, fencing, skydiving, and table-tennis; various types of music (classical, heavy metal, oldies, folk, religious, funk, etc.); politics, such topics as U.S., Europe, India, equality, sex, and correctness; buying and selling of most anything; movies, soap operas, and fans of celebrities, such as David Letterman, Madonna, Bill Gates, Rush Limbaugh, Howard Stern, and the Disney characters. There is also a very large collection of groups related to computers and computing—from hardware and software to programming, game playing, graphics, pictures, and research.

Although many people consider the Usenet to be the Internet, that just isn't true. The Internet is a totally separate system. The Usenet is available on the Internet; it is also available at many other sites that are *not* on the Internet.

You may have experience with other discussion-type groups. If so, don't make the social blunder of calling *newsgroups* (or just *groups*) by any other name, such

overview / email / **newsgroups** / mailing lists / telnet / ftp as *forums*, *BBSs* (for bulletin board systems), *SIGs* (for special interest groups), or *conferences*. You will be regarded as an ignorant *newbie*. Note: The term *newbie*, for someone new to the net, is not necessarily derogatory. But *ignorant newbie* and *clueless newbie* are definitely derogatory.

The Organization of Usenet Newsgroups

Newsgroups are organized into hierarchies and named to show their location. There are seven "official" Usenet top-level names, plus many others. Here are the most widely distributed hierarchies:

The original seven hierarchies:

comp	computers and related topics
misc	miscellaneous topics that don't fit anywhere else
news	topics and announcements about the Usenet itself
rec	recreation, hobbies, and games
sci	science-related topics
soc	social groups, both socializing and social interests, many ethnic groups
talk	discussions and arguments, often about politics

Additional hierarchies, not carried by all sites:

alt	unusual or controversial subjects
bionet	research biology
bit	bitnet information and topics on bitnet mailing lists
biz	business
clari	Clarinet News, a commercial online news provider
gnu	a UNIX alternative
info	information on some diverse subjects
k12	K-12 students and teachers
relcom	Russian language groups
vmsnet	users of DEC's VMS operating system

Moderated vs. Free-for-All Groups

In most groups, anyone can post anything he wishes. But moderated groups are different; only the moderator (a person) can post to a moderated group. To reply to an article, or post your own, send it to the moderator, who will decide which articles to post. The discussions in moderated groups usually remain on-topic (unlike some unmoderated groups).

News Reader Software

In order to read and respond to the news, you must have news reader software. The news reader program must be installed either on your own computer station or on your local host computer.

You already know there are many different mail reader programs; now you'll find that the same is true for news reader programs. There are lots. And new, improved programs are developed regularly. Therefore, we can't just list the commands here for all mail readers; instead, we'll look at the functions that you need to be able to perform. You can write the commands for your mail reader program on the Usenet Command Reference page (page 23).

Basically, you need to be able to read newsgroup articles and to respond to them if you wish. Any other tasks are "bells and whistles." Some of the nice extras include the ability to exclude news that doesn't interest you and being able to follow a *thread*, a topic of conversation, without having to manually search for the articles.

Reading Newsgroup Postings

All news reader software provides a method to select a newsgroup and read the articles. You can choose to view a list of the article headers (containing the name of the poster and the subject line), or just begin reading the first article. Unless you have *lots* of time, you will want to view the headers and be selective about the articles you read. (This is where good subject lines pay off.)

Your news reader software will keep track of the articles you have read. The next time you return to the group, you should see only the new articles.

Following a Thread
When you read an interesting article, you'll want to read any replies to the article—rather than wade through a bunch of other topics first. Most software will allow you to follow a thread so that you can read all the replies to the current topic

Ignoring Articles
There are two ways to eliminate articles that don't interest you. The first is manual: You scan the list of headers and mark uninteresting topics as if you had read them. That way, the articles won't appear on your next visit. With the right news reader program (such as trn), you can create a file holding topics (or the ID of

people) that you don't want cluttering your screen. The file, called a *Kill* file, can speed your reading.

Saving Articles

When you find an interesting article that you want to keep, you can save it on your own computer system. The format and location of the saved file varies, depending on your computer setup.

Responding to Newsgroup Posting

When you read something interesting, you may decide that you want to add your opinion to the discussion. You can send a reply to the group (called a *follow-up*), or send it to the author of the original article (called a *reply*). If you think that the thousands of folks reading the group will be interested in your reply, send a follow-up. Otherwise, it's a good idea to reply directly to the author.

When you follow up or reply, you will probably want to quote the portion of the original article to which you are responding. Your news reader software may insert the message automatically, or you may have to request it. Be sure to delete the irrelevant parts; include only as much of the original article as necessary for readers to know what you are responding to. (Refer to "Replying to

Messages," in chapter 2, for more information about quoting the original message.)

Newsgroup Frequently Asked Questions (FAQ) Files

Before you send off a question to a newsgroup, you need to do a little homework. There are some questions that are asked over and over, and people get tired of answering them. So *many* groups have created a file of the frequently asked questions—called a FAQ file. A group's FAQ file is usually reposted to the newsgroup periodically, so search for it. However, since different sites expire their news at different times, you may not find the FAQ file in the group when you look. However, you can find most FAQs in the news.answers group. Also, in chapter 6 you will learn to retrieve FAQ files from a site that keeps an archive copy of most FAQs.

Usenet Etiquette

Do:

- Reread the email etiquette section. Usenet posters are also human beings, with feelings.
- Include the original message when replying to an article. Make sure to delete all but the relevant lines.

- Remember that many people must pay for the messages they read. Keep your messages short and concise, and do not include long, fancy signatures.

Don't

- Flame. *Flaming* is sending nasty responses. Sometimes people send increasingly nasty words back and forth, generating "flame wars." Some individuals try to incite flaming with outrageous statements, called "flame bait." Don't stoop to their level by responding.

Abbreviations

Net veterans use many abbreviations. Here are some of the more common ones; there are more in the glossary at the end of this guide, and more yet in some of the FAQ files you will find on the net.

BTW	by the way
BTA	but then again
IMHO	in my humble opinion
LOL	laughing out loud
ROTFL	rolling on the floor laughing
FOAF	friend of a friend
FWIW	for what it's worth

Try This

- Read the articles in `news.announce.newusers`. You will find many articles of interest to new users.
- Make sure to read the FAQ: `Answers to Frequently Asked Questions about Usenet` (in `news.announce.newusers`)
- Scan the list of articles in `news.answers`. Find an interesting FAQ file and save it on your own system.
- Check the articles in `alt.internet.services`. If you are looking for a particular service on the Internet, this is the place to ask.
- Pick a newsgroup interesting to you, read an article, and follow the thread of the conversation.
- Send a test message to `alt.test` or `misc.test`. Give it a subject of `test` with anything you want as a message. Then be prepared for lots of responses, from various parts of the world. Be sure to notice the routing that your messages took. In the future, use a subject of `test-ignore`, and the automatic test answering programs will not respond, but you will be able to see your test

message posted in the newsgroup. (Only post test messages in the two test groups.)

- Find a conversation thread that interests you, and send a reply to the person who posted the article. (Reply, don't follow up.)
- Locate another interesting conversation, or a question that you know the answer to, and send a follow-up message. You will be able to see your reply posted in the newsgroup later. The delay depends on many factors and can vary from a few minutes to several hours.

Usenet Problems

If you have problems with Usenet, try:

- Read the screen, looking for Help. You may be able to look up instructions online. Try h or ? or help or F1 to find help.

- Is the command uppercase or lowercase? Case counts on some systems (notably UNIX).
- Read the manual. Your manual may be stored online. Try

    man *programname* (use the name of your news reader program).
- Ask someone around you for help.
- Send email to your local system administrator. If your problem concerns your local mail program or system setup, try to solve it locally.
- As a last resort, post a question to the group news.software.readers. It is likely that someone will have an answer. Do *not* post a news reader question in any other group.

Usenet Command Reference   (page 1 of 2)
Name of your news reader program _____

Command (Working with Groups)	trn and rn news readers	Your news reader program
Launch news reader program	rn or trn	
Exit news reader program (while working with newsgroups)	q	
Go to a group	g *groupname* (also subscribes you to the group)	
Subscribe to a group	Same as above	
Enter the next group with unread articles	y or Spacebar	
Unsubscribe from a group	u	
List available newsgroups	l	
Go to previous group with unread messages	p	
(Working with Articles)		
Show titles of unread articles	=	
Read next article	Spacebar	
Follow a thread	(trn only) Ctrl+n (next reply) Ctrl+p (previous article)	
Scroll to next page of article	Spacebar (goes to next article if at end of article)	

Usenet Command Reference (page 2 of 2)

Command (Working with Articles)	trn and rn news readers	Your news reader program
Skip this article	n	
Skip (kill) all related articles	k	
Kill all related articles permanently	K	
Reply to the author of an article (do not include text of original message)	r	
Reply to the author of an article (include text of original message)	R	
Follow up to an article (do not include text of original)	f	
Follow up to an article (include text of original message)	F	
Save an article in a file	s *filename*	
Mark all articles as read (catch up)	c	
Exit this group	q	
Exit articles (return to newsgroup selection)	q	
Help	h	

overview / email / **newsgroups** / mailing lists / telnet / ftp

RECEIVING INFORMATION FROM MAILING LISTS

Using Mailing Lists

Finding Mailing Lists

Subscribing to Mailing Lists

Responding to Mailing List Postings

Unsubscribing from Mailing Lists

Requesting More Information

Try This

Mailing List Problems

Mailing List Command Reference

Using Mailing Lists

Mailing lists, like newsgroups, are used for carrying on discussions. However, mailing list messages come directly to your mail in-basket. The discussion comes to you, rather than the other way around.

You can subscribe to a mailing list by sending an email message to the maintainer of the list. Once you have subscribed, all messages mailed to the list are sent to you.

Some lists are maintained by software, others are maintained manually. Two programs that automate subscription lists, *listserv* and *majordomo*, send the messages automatically and immediately. For manually maintained lists, a person maintains the subscription list and forwards all messages to subscribers. You can guess which method is faster.

Just like newsgroups, some lists are moderated, others are not. When a list is moderated, your messages go to the moderator, who decides which messages to post. Moderated lists tend to stick to the topic better than unmoderated lists—which you may or may not prefer.

Some mailing lists are affiliated with a newsgroup, and messages are posted both places. One advantage of using a mailing list is that you will be sure to receive all messages, even if you are gone for awhile. And there are many people who have access to email, but not to Usenet newsgroups.

Finding Mailing Lists

There are thousands of mailing lists available. You can find listings of mailing lists in various places on the Internet. Look in the newsgroup `news.announce.newusers` for a file called something like *Publicly Accessible Mailing Lists*. You can also send an email message requesting a list of *all* listserv-managed lists, or for only the lists matching a topic that you specify. For example, send an email message

```
To: listserv@bitnic.educom.edu
```

Do not include a subject line, but write a one-line message:

```
list global/<topic>
```

Examples:

`list global/med`	List of all groups containing "med."
`list global/politic`	List of all groups containing "politic."
`list global`	List of *all* groups. (Watch out, the list is *very* long.)

You can include more than one command in a message, but each must appear on a separate line:

```
list global/jazz
list global/classical music
```

Subscribing to Mailing Lists

You subscribe to a mailing list by sending a request to the maintainer of the list. For lists maintained by listserv or majordomo, your request goes to the listserv or majordomo address. For other lists, send your request to `listname-request@listaddress`. For example, to subscribe to the mailing list for collecting trading cards, called `cards`, send this request:

```
To: cards-request@tanstaafl.uchicago.edu
```

Do not include a subject line, but write a one-line message:

```
subscribe Yourname@Youraddress
```

(Include your full email address.)

After you receive a confirmation that you have been added to the list, send your messages to the list name:

```
To: cards@tanstaafl.uchicago.edu
```

Make sure to include a meaningful subject line when you post messages; your message will be delivered to all subscribers of the list.

For listserv-maintained lists, send your subscription request to the `listserv@address`. For example, to subscribe to the list called `upnews`, which holds discussions of electronic music, send this message:

> To: listserv@vm.marist.edu

Do not include a subject line, but write a one-line message:

> subscribe upnews *Yourfirstname Yourlastname*

(Note: No email address is required; listserv takes your address from your email header.)

When you post messages to the list, send your messages:

> To: upnews@vm.marist.edu

Include a meaningful subject line and your message.

Responding to Mailing List Postings
You will find the list postings in your mail in-basket. So it follows that you use your mail program to respond. Depending on the nature of your reply, you may send your response to the entire list or only to the original poster of the message. If the topic seems to be a running discussion, with group participation, send the reply to the list. However, don't send replies to the entire list when the topic is of limited interest or when you are responding to a specific question from an individual.

Make sure to notice the `Reply to:` header in the original message; usually the replies should go to the requested address. However, you may ignore the `Reply to:` and choose your own destination. Your mail program will provide a way to change the destination address; you may need to investigate the manual or Help to find the command.

Unsubscribing from Mailing Lists
When you decide to unsubscribe from a mailing list, you send the request to the maintainer of the list—not the list itself. (You don't want to send your request to everyone on the list.) Using the example groups subscribed to earlier (`cards` and `upnews`), unsubscribe by sending a message:

> To: cards-request@tanstaafl.uchicago.edu

Do not include a subject line, but write a one-line message:

> unsubscribe *Yourname@Youraddress*

For the `upnews` list, send your message:

    To: listserv@vm.marist.edu

Do not include a subject line, but include a one-line message:

    unsubscribe upnews

Note: When you communicate with a list maintained by listserv or majordomo, you must name the list in your message. The listserv/majordomo software at one site generally maintains multiple lists, so you specify the one you want. But an address such as `cards-request` is only for the `cards` mailing list, so you do not name the list in the message.

Requesting More Information

Listserv software has many additional commands available. For example, you can request an index of previous topics or a list of all subscribed members, or you can make your name unlisted, so that it doesn't appear in the subscription list. If you want a list of commands, send your request to the list maintainer (the `listserv` address), with a single-line message of `info refcard`.

Try This

- Using your mail reader software, find a list of mailing lists in `news.announce.newusers`. Read the list and find one that interests you.
- Send an email message to find a mailing list on a subject of your choice. Send the message to `listserv@bitnic.educom.edu`, with no subject line, and a one-line message of `list global/topic` (replace `topic` with the topic of your choice).
- Subscribe to a mailing list of your choice.
- After you receive a confirmation message from the list maintainer, send for a list of mailing list commands.
- Subscribe to the Internet Roadmap:
  Send an email message to:

      listserv@ua1vm.ua.edu

  with a single-line message of

      subscribe roadmap firstname lastname

  (Fill in your own first and last names, of course.)

- Subscribe to one of these lists.
                    (Send request to:)

  For news and information about the Internet:
  announce   `majordomo@radio.com`
                  `subscribe announce`

  Philosophy:
  `belief-l`   `listserv@brownvm.brown.edu`
                  `subscribe belief-l` *your full name*

  Interesting things available on the Internet:
  `scout-report` `majordomo@is.internic.net`
                  `subscribe scout-report`

  Cinema:
  `cinema-l`   `listserv@american.edu`
                  `subscribe cinema-l` *name*
                  (use your full name)

  Computer games:
  `games-l`   `listserv@brownvm.brown.edu`
                  `subscribe games-l` *your full name*

  Scuba diving:
  `scuba-l`   `listserv@brownvm.brown.edu`
                  `subscribe scuba-l` *your full name*

Mailing List Problems

If you have problems with mailing lists, try these tactics:

- Make sure all requests (subscribe, unsubscribe, info) go the maintainer of the list, not the list itself. For listserv lists, use `listserv@`*siteaddress*; for majordomo lists, use `majordomo@`*siteaddress*; for other lists, use *listname*`-request@`*siteaddress*.
- Make sure that your email software is not automatically appending a signature to your email messages.
- Many lists have bitnet addresses, which are available only on the bitnet network. Unless you are located at an educational institution that is on bitnet, look for an Internet-style address (such as one ending in `.edu`).

Mailing List Command Reference

Listserv and majordomo lists **Send email message to** listserv@*siteaddress* or majordomo@*siteaddress*	Send email message with no subject line and a one-line message
Subscribe	subscribe *listname yourfirstname lastname*
Unsubscribe	unsubscribe *listname* or signoff *listname*
Send for a list of information topics	info
Send for a list of commands	info refcard
Non-listserv/majordomo mailing lists **Send email message to** *listname*-request@*siteaddress*	Send email message with no subject line and a one-line message
Subscribe	subscribe *yourmail@address*
Unsubscribe	unsubscribe *yourmail@address*
Send for a list of commands	Varies by list Usually help or info

TELNETTING TO OTHER COMPUTER SITES

Logging On to Other Computer Sites

Understanding Terminal Babel

Issuing Telnet Commands

Finding Sites to Telnet To

Try This

Telnet Problems

Telnet Command Reference

Logging On to Other Computer Sites

You can use the telnet command to log on to remote computer sites. You can telnet to any computer on which you have an ID and password, and access your account there. In addition, many sites allow guests to log on, with access to limited resources.

There are many gems on remote systems that you can access using telnet, such as library catalogs and databases. You can log on to the Library of Congress, as well as many other libraries, all around the world. You can find databases for agriculture, aviation, geography, history, medicine, outer space, book reviews, magazine articles, and many more.

When you use telnet, you are again using the services of a *client* and a *server*. Your own local host computer must have a telnet client program, which makes a request. The remote site must have a server program, which provides the service (in response to the requests). You will type commands to your local client, such as to open a connection to a remote computer. After you connect to the remote computer, you will issue commands for that system.

Understanding Terminal Babel

Unfortunately, there are many different types of computer terminals, including PCs and Macs, attached to many different types of computers. When you connect to a remote host, chances are that your terminal type is different from that system's terminals. Some terminals transmit each character as it is typed, some transmit a line at a time, and some (notably IBM mainframe terminals) transmit a screenfull only when you press the Enter key or a program function key (PF key). Also, different terminals use many different control codes to determine row and column placement on the screen, for software that uses a full-screen display.

In an attempt to standardize, most computers recognize their own local terminal type, plus the DEC VT100. (Some computers also recognize a few other common terminal types.) Although you probably don't have a VT100, you can usually make your terminal act like (*emulate*) a VT100. Check your software (the menus, Help, the manual) for *Terminal Emulation*; when you find VT100, select it. Another very common terminal type is ANSI (for American National Standards Institute), which is somewhat similar to VT100. For some systems, ANSI terminal emulation may work

better for you than VT100. Be prepared to experiment a little.

Issuing Telnet Commands

It's easy to begin a telnet session—just type `telnet` and the name of the remote computer. For example, to telnet to the Library of Congress, type:

```
telnet locis.loc.gov
```

Or, on most systems, you can just type:

```
telnet
```

The local telnet client program begins and issues a prompt, where you can type a telnet command. The command to open a connection to a remote site is `open sitename`.

```
telnet
telnet> open locis.loc.gov
```

Or, if you're really lucky, it may be easier yet. If you are using a computer that uses windowing or menus, you may be able to just select an icon or a menu option to begin a telnet session.

Connecting to the Remote Computer

Usually, you will connect to the remote computer and receive a *Connected* message. Likely you will also see something like `Escape character is '^]'`. *Write this down,* you may need it soon! What it means is that you can type Ctrl+] (Ctrl and the right bracket) to escape from the server software, in order to issue a command to your local client. This is sometimes the only way out, if the remote system quits responding to you.

Logging On to the Remote Computer
The majority of computers will ask you to login once you are connected. For some computers, you must have an established account to login; for others, you can login with your own name, or with a guest ID. (Many references that list telnet sites also provide you with a login ID and password.)

Once you have logged on to a remote computer, you are just another user on that system. It's just as if you had logged on from a terminal attached to that computer. If you have logged on to your own account somewhere, you can proceed to read your mail and do any other tasks that you normally do on the system. If you are logged on to a strange system, you will have to use commands that system understands. Fortunately, most systems either display menus for you or show how to get Help, along the bottom of the screen.

Logging Off the Remote Computer
Sometimes it's easier to get on to a remote system than to get off. Your first choice should be to politely log off the system. If there is a menu choice, use that. Otherwise, try `q`, `quit`, `exit`, `Ctrl+d`, or `done`. If you can't get out, press `Ctrl+]`, which should escape to your local telnet client; then type `quit` or `close`. (Your telnet client will "hang up on them.")

More about Terminal Differences
One problem that occurs occasionally: The characters you type do not appear on your screen; or, every letter appears twice. The solution is the same for both: Press `Ctrl+]` to enter command mode for your local client, and type `set echo`. Then press Enter to return to the remote computer.

Connecting to a Port Address
When you find the name of a system to telnet to, sometimes it is followed by a port number. The remote computer can tell what service you want by the port number you specify. Often you won't be required to have a login ID or password if you use an assigned port number. If you find a port number after a computer name, type the number on the telnet command,

following the computer name. For example, to use the geography database at the University of Michigan (at port 3000), type:

```
telnet martini.eecs.umich.edu 3000
```

Finding Sites to Telnet To

There are several good sources for telnet sites. One good source is books, such as the Internet Yellow Pages (authors: Harley Hahn and Rick Stout, from Osborne McGraw-Hill).

On the Internet, you can usually find information about new telnet sites in alt.internet.services and alt.bbs.internet. There are some good lists available, generally available by ftp (which is covered in chapter 6). You will also find some good telnet sites when you use gopher (chapter 8) and veronica (chapter 9).

Scott Yanoff regularly posts a list of many sources on the Internet. You need ftp to retrieve his list. See the "Try This" section in chapter 6.

Another good resource is EFF's *Guide to the Internet* (formerly *The Big Dummy's Guide to the Internet*), also available by ftp.

Hytelnet
One of the really good systems you can telnet to is *hytelnet*. Hytelnet is actually a program, available in several locations, which automates the process of accessing libraries, databases, and bibliographies. When you explore with hytelnet, you will find listings of hundreds of other telnet sites. See the "Try This" section for hytelnet instructions.

Try This

- Retrieve the correct time of day, in Mountain Standard Time, from the federal atomic clock in Colorado. Telnet to india.colorado.edu 13 (make sure to include the 13). You will be given the correct time and disconnected.
- Retrieve a weather forecast from the University of Michigan's Department of Atmospheric, Oceanographic and Space Sciences. Telnet to madlab.sprl.umich.edu 3000 (make sure to include the 3000).
- Search a database. Try one of these: geography: martini.eecs.umich.edu 3000

ham radio

call signs: `ns.risc.net`
login: `hamradio`
health: `fdabbs.fda.gov`
login: `bbs`

You'll be asked for your name and a password that you can use in the future. After entering both, type `topics`.

environment: `envirolink.org`
login: `gopher`

interest rates, foreign exchange rates, price indexes, statistics:
`ebb.stat-usa.gov`
login: `guest`

land use, geological info about US:
`glis.cr.usgs.gov`
login: `guest`

- Explore using hytelnet. You can search university and library catalogs, and find telnet addresses for many databases. Telnet to `access.usask.ca` and login as `hytelnet`. Or, you can telnet to `info.ccit.arizona.edu`, or `laguna.epcc.edu` (login: `library`).

Telnet Problems

If you have trouble with telnet, try these tactics:

- Make sure you can emulate a VT100 terminal. Ask your local system administrator if you are unsure.
- The site you are calling may be an IBM mainframe. Your clues are the letters VM or MVS (names of IBM operating systems) and lots of uppercase characters. If you think the site is an IBM mainframe, try using a program called tn3270 in place of telnet. The tn3270 program emulates an IBM 3270 terminal and will make the response much better.
- If the site you are calling *from* is an IBM mainframe, you have a different problem. Ask your system administrator about the ANET program, which allows your terminal to emulate a VT100. IBM terminals send data only when the Enter key or a PF key is pressed; most computers expect to receive individual characters as they are typed. You will have to fool both the mainframe and the remote site to make it read single characters and cursor-movement keys.

- The remote site seems to refuse the connection. This can happen for several reasons. The site may be down for maintenance or problems. Also, many sites don't allow connections during certain hours, especially during their busiest hours. Or, you may have forgotten to use the port number, which can cause the connection to fail.
- Your typing disappears. You need to set the echo on. Press the escape character (usually Ctrl+]), type set echo, and press Enter to return to the remote host.

- Everything you type appears twice. You need the same solution as for the previous problem (set echo).
- The remote host asks for an ID and a password, and you don't have an account. First check your reference—should you use a port number? Then, check to see if you were supplied with an ID and/ or a password in your reference. You can try logging in with your own name as the ID and password; also try guest for the ID. As a last resort, you can call the site and ask for instructions.

Telnet Command Reference

Action	Command
Launch telnet and connect to remote site	`telnet sitename` `telnet sitename portnumber`
Launch telnet	`telnet`
(From telnet> prompt:)	
Exit telnet	`quit` or `exit`
Connect to a telnet site	`open siteaddress` `open siteaddress portnumber`
Select a new escape character	`set escape character` (type the character you want to use)
View Help	`?`
Turn echo on or off (toggle)	`set echo`
Set terminal to send a line at a time	`mode line`
Return to remote host from telnet> prompt	`Enter`
(From remote host)	
Escape to local telnet client (to get `telnet>` prompt)	Press escape character, usually `Ctrl +]`
Log off remote host	`quit`, `exit`, `Ctrl+d`, or `done`

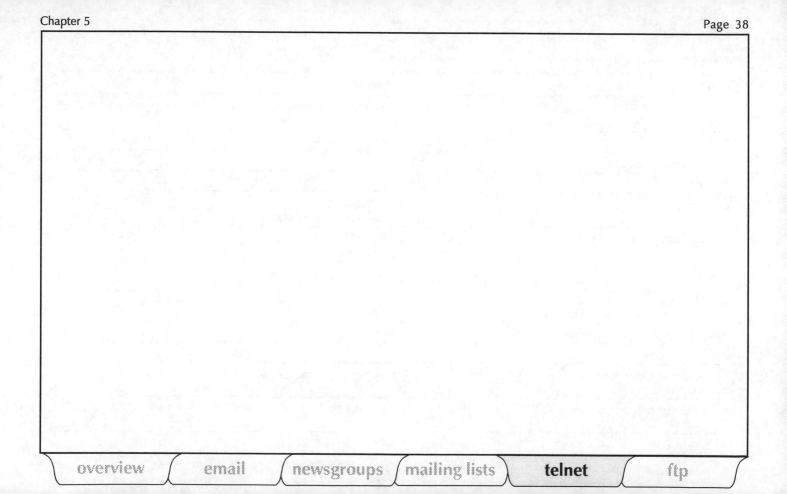

Transferring Files Using Ftp

Using Ftp to Retrieve Files from Other Computers

Using Anonymous Ftp

Searching the Directories for the Files You Want

Transferring Files

Signing Off

Try This

Ftp Problems

Ftp Command Reference

Using Ftp to Retrieve Files from Other Computers

Millions of files, stored on individual computers all around the Internet, are yours for the taking. You can find shareware programs that run on your own computer, weather maps, the complete text of the Congressional Record, recipes, books, pictures, and sounds. The many FAQ (frequently asked questions) files are available by ftp (file transfer protocol), as well as several guidebooks for new users.

To use ftp, you run a client program on your host computer, which connects and logs you on to a remote site. After the connection is made, you communicate with the remote site using ftp commands. You can view and change directories, locate the files you want, and copy the files to your host. Although the computers on the Internet use many different operating systems, file structures, and commands, they all "speak" ftp (with an occasional strange dialect).

If you have an account on another computer, you can use ftp to log on. You will have the same rights to directories and files that you would if you were logged on locally. However, most of the files you want will be on computers on which you *don't* have an account.

Fortunately, most sites allow for *anonymous* users, with access limited to certain directories and files.

Using Anonymous Ftp

To launch ftp on your host computer, look around; you may have a menu item or an icon to select. When you launch the program, it will ask you the name of the host to connect to. If you don't have a menu item or an icon, type in the command

> `ftp` *sitename*   (using the actual name of the remote site, of course).

Assuming all goes well, you will be given a message that the connection was made, and a request for your name. Don't type your name—that's not really what it wants. Instead, type `anonymous`. You will then be prompted for a password; type your full email address (it won't appear on the screen). Note: Some sites check for a valid email address, but most don't. You are providing the information as a courtesy, since you are using their system.

Example: An Anonymous ftp Login:
(Bold text indicates the characters typed from the keyboard.)
> **ftp ftp.csd.uwm.edu**
> Connecting to ftp.csd.uwm.edu 129.89.7.202, port 21

```
220 alpha2.csd.uwm.edu FTP server (Version wu-2.4(3)
Wed Jun 22 17:23:50 CDT
199 ready.USER (identify yourself to the host):
anonymous
>>>USER anonymous
Guest login ok, send your complete e-mail address as
password.
Password:
(email address—does not show on screen)
>>>PASS ********
230-University of Wisconsin-Milwaukee FTP server
230-Local time is Thu Sep  8 23:03:00 1994
230-
230-If you have any unusual problems, please report them
230-via e-mail to help@uwm.edu.
230-
230-If you do have problems, please try using a dash (-) as
the
230-first character of your password – this will turn off
the
230-continuation messages that may be confusing your ftp
client.
230-
230-Please read the file Policy
230-it was last modified on Mon Jan 24 12:49:58 1994 - 227
days ago
30 Guest login ok, access restrictions apply.
Command:
```

The `Command:` prompt indicates you are logged in, and the ftp program is awaiting a command. Note: On some systems, you will see `ftp>` in place of `Command:`.

Searching the Directories for the Files You Want

Sometimes you will know exactly the filename and directory you need, but usually you want to look around and see what files are available. The commands you use are ftp commands, but since the original Internet computers all used UNIX, ftp commands are *very* similar to UNIX commands. The most useful commands are:

cd   Change working directory on the remote site

lcd   Change working directory on your local host

dir   Display a listing of the current directory (on the remote site)

ls -l   Same as dir command

ls -CF Display the current directory, filenames only, in columns (similar to /w on MS-DOS dir command)

One very important note: For the majority of sites, the case (uppercase or lowercase) is *very important*. You won't get the same results using -c and -C. This is because most computers on the Internet use some variety of UNIX; and in UNIX, all commands, filenames, and directory names are case sensitive.

Example: Displaying a Directory Listing

```
dir
>>>PORT 140,144,202,50,18,30
200 PORT command successful.
>>>LIST
150 Opening ASCII mode data connection for /bin/ls.
total 9
------     1 root  system     0 Oct 29 1993  .notar
------     1 root  system     0 Oct 29 1993  .rhosts
-r-r-r-    1 root  users   2148 Jan 24 1994  Policy
d-x-x-x    2 root  system   512 Mar 25 08:29 bin
d-x-x-x    4 root  system   512 Mar 25 08:29 etc
d-wxrwxrwx 2 ftp   system   512 Sep 08 00:53 incoming
dr-xrwxrwt 29 root system  1024 Sep 08 16:49 pub
d-x-x-x    2 root  system    12 Mar 25 08:29 sbin
d-x-x-x    5 root  system   512 Mar 25 08:29 usr
226 Transfer complete.
Command:
```

Although this is way more than you wanted to know, some of the information is very useful. The first character of each entry (d or -) indicates whether it is a directory (d) or file (-). The rightmost item is the name of the file or directory. In between, you can find the date and time of last update, as well as the file's size, in bytes (roughly equivalent to the number of characters).

Changing Directories
The command to change to another directory is `cd` .
You can change to a subdirectory of the current
directory, or, by giving the complete path, change to
any directory.

`cd pub`	(Change to pub, a subdirectory of the current directory)
`cd pub/misc`	(Change to the misc subdirectory of the pub directory)

Viewing the Directory Listing
If the list scrolls by too fast to read, try one of these
commands (results differ by site):

> `ls -CF` (watch the case, it matters)
> or `ls -l"|more"`
> or `ls -l|more`
> or `Ctrl+s` to stop scrolling, `Ctrl+q` to resume

Transferring Files
The files you plan to transfer come in several different
varieties and require different techniques for copying.
Some files are text (called ASCII, for the coding
method usually used for storing text). The files that
aren't text may be executable programs, graphic

images, or compressed files. For text files, you must
transfer in ASCII mode; for all other files, you must
transfer in *binary* mode (also called *image* mode).
Unfortunately, the ftp program doesn't figure this out
for you; you must determine the type and set the
mode before transferring the file. If you transfer in the
wrong mode, the file will still copy to your system—but
it will be scrambled and unusable.

Selecting the Mode
From the directory listing you will find clues indicating
the file type. All `readme` and `index` files are text, as well
as any file that has `text` or `txt` as part of its name.
Filenames that end in `exe`, `zip`, `z`, `Z`, `gz`, `gif`, `jpg`, `tar`,
`hqz`, or `sit` must be transferred in binary mode. For
any other file, you will have to look for other clues.
When in doubt, try binary first.

Notice the filenames in the directory listing following
this paragraph. These files hold the *Guide to the
Internet* from EFF (the Electronic Frontier Foundation).
You may have heard of this excellent guide, which was
formerly called *The Big Dummy's Guide to the
Internet*. (FYI: These files are found at `ftp.eff.org` in
the `/pub/Net_info/EFF_Net_Guide` directory.)

```
-rw-r—r—  1 mech  doc    37377 Mar  9 03:34 netgd2_2.zip
-rw-r—r—  1 mech  doc   394870 Aug 3 17:23 netguide.eff
-rw-r—r—  1 mech  mech   52543 Jun  1 19:36 netguide.faq
```

The first two files in the list hold the guide, and the third file is a faq (frequently asked questions) file. The first file (netgd2_2.zip) is a compressed file and must be transferred in binary mode. The second file (netguide.eff) and third file (netguide.faq) are both text and should be transferred in ASCII mode. The first two files hold the same information; you can choose to transfer one or the other. Notice the difference in file size. Of course, the compressed file will transfer much more quickly than the text file. If you transfer the compressed file, you will need a program to decompress it (unzip or pkunzip, in this case). Compression/Decompression programs are also available for transfer by ftp. The commands to select the mode are:

ascii	ASCII (text) mode
binary (or image)	binary mode

Getting a File

After you have selected the transfer mode, you can transfer a file, using the get command. Be careful when you type in the name of the file to transfer; usually the case is significant. That is, Readme is not the same file as readme or README.

```
Command:                 (prompt: waiting for a command)
ascii                    (set to ASCII mode for text transfer)
200 Type set to A.       (message generated by ftp program)
Command:                 (prompt: waiting for a command)
get netguide.faq         (command to transfer the file)
150 Opening ASCII mode data connection
              for netguide.faq (52543
              bytes)
226 Transfer complete
Command:                 (prompt: waiting for the next
                          command)
```

In this example, we'll do a binary mode transfer of a file, giving the new file a different name from the original:

```
Command:                 (prompt: waiting for a
                          command)
binary                   (set to binary mode)
200 Type set to I.       (response from ftp, using
                          binary/image mode)
Command:                 (prompt: waiting for
                          another command)
get netgd2_2.zip guide.zip  (transfer the file, renaming
                          the copy)
150 Opening BINARY mode data connection
              for netgd2_2.zip
              (xxxxx bytes)
226 Transfer complete    (responses from remote
                          site)
Command:                 (ready for the next
                          command)
```

Sometimes you need to rename the file as you copy it. The filename on the remote system may not be a legal filename on your computer. Or, perhaps you want the filename to be more meaningful to you later, or you might already have a file with that name (common with a filename like `readme`). To give the new file a different name, just add the new filename to the end of the `get` command.

```
get filename newfilename
```

Choosing the Location for a New File
When you transfer a file to your system, the file will appear in the directory that was current at the time you launched ftp. If you would like to change the current directory on your local system, use the `lcd` command (for local change working directory).

```
lcd \newstuff
```
(change to the \newstuff directory on the local system)

Transferring Multiple Files
You can transfer multiple files with the `mget` command (for multiple get). It's legal to name several filenames on the command line and to use wildcards to specify groups of files. One warning: Wildcards behave differently on different systems. In UNIX, `mus*` would match all filenames beginning with `mus`, including those with periods (such as `music`, `muscles.gif`, and

`mushy.txt`). On MS-DOS systems, you would need `mus*.*` to match those filenames with periods.

```
mget file1 file2 file3   (transfer the 3 named files)
mget fil*                (transfer all files beginning
                          with fil)
```

Note that you cannot give the files new names when you use the `mget` command.

Using Compressed Files
Often the files you find will be compressed, using one of several different compression methods. Compressed files require less storage space and take less time to transfer. You will need to recognize the various compression methods, and have the proper decompression software, in order to use the files. Note: You can find the compress/decompress software on the Internet, and ftp it to your system, if need be. You'll be able to find the needed programs using archie (chapter 7) or with veronica (chapter 9). Refer to chapter 14 for help in downloading and decompressing files.

Suffix	File Type
.Z	UNIX compressed file. Use `uncompress` to decompress the file.
.z	UNIX packed file. Use `unpack` to decompress the file.

.zip	PKZIPed file. Use `pkunzip` (available for many different systems, including MS-DOS and Windows).
.gz	UNIX zipped file. Use `gzip` or `gunzip` to decompress the file.
.sit	Macintosh StuffIt file. Use `UnStuffIt` program to decompress the file.
.hqx	Macintosh compressed file. Use `BinHex` program to decompress the file.

You can save yourself some trouble if you are transferring UNIX compressed files (`.Z` or `.z`) to a non-UNIX site. If you drop the extension from the filename, the ftp program will decompress the file before sending it. In that case, do an ASCII mode transfer—the file will be text. For example, you want the compressed file, `Index.z`. You can do a binary transfer of `Index.z`, and decompress it after transfer; or, you can do a text transfer, calling the file `Index` (without the `.z` extension).

Command:	(prompt: waiting for a command)
`ascii`	(set to ASCII for text transfer)
`200 Type set to A.`	(message generated by ftp program)
Command:	(prompt: waiting for a command)
`get Index`	(command to decompress and transfer the file)

```
150 Opening ASCII mode data connection for
Index (1520 bytes)
226 Transfer complete
```

Command:	(prompt: waiting for the next command)

Reading Readme and Index Files
Many directories hold a readme file and/or an index file; you will easily recognize them by their names. Generally, you will transfer the files to your local host and read them there. On some systems, you can read a file by directing it to your screen, rather than to a file. Try this:

get *filename* -	(if your local site is using UNIX)
get *filename* tt	(if your local site is using VMS)
get *filename* con	(if your local site is MS-DOS)

On some systems, you can type:

get filename |more	(Pauses when the screen is full. Press the Spacebar to resume, or q to cancel the listing.)

Signing Off

When you're finished rooting around and transferring files, the command is `quit` or `close`.

```
Command:      (prompt: waiting for a command)
quit          (tell ftp you're ready to quit)
>>>QUIT       (response from ftp program)
221 Goodbye.  (response from ftp program)
```

Try This

- Retrieve the file that holds answers to commonly asked "New Internet User" questions.

ftp to this site:	`nis.nsf.net`
Login as:	`anonymous`
Password:	*your email address*
Change directory:	`cd documents/rfc`
Set the mode:	`ascii`
Transfer the file:	`get rfc1325.txt`
Get their index too:	`get INDEX.rfc`
Say goodbye:	`quit`

- Retrieve a faq (frequently asked questions) file for a newsgroup of your choice, from the archives at MIT.

  Anonymous ftp to `rtfm.mit.edu` and change to this directory:

  ```
  /pub/usenet/news.answers
  ```

  Give a dir command, and select a faq file that interests you. Note: if the directory listing scrolls too fast to read, see "Viewing the Directory Listing," page 42. Be sure to use ASCII mode for the transfer.

- Retrieve the Internet Services List (known as "Yanoff's List").

  Anonymous ftp to `ftp.csd.uwm.edu`, change to the `/pub` directory, and `get inet.services.txt`.

- Ftp to Microsoft Corporation's server (`ftp.microsoft.com`), login as `anonymous`, and retrieve their index file (`index.txt`). Then change to the `Softlib` directory, and get `README.TXT` and another file called `index.txt` (the index for this directory). You will have to give `index.txt` a new name on your system, since you already have a file with that name (`get index.txt newname`).

- If you are a Macintosh user, you need the Internet Tour stack, as well as the utility programs for archiving and compressing files. Ftp to `ftp.io.com` and change to the directory `/pub/io/utilities/mac`. Then do an ASCII transfer of `00readme.txt` and `mac.arcer.guide`. Quit from ftp and read both files. Then ftp back to `ftp.io.com` and retrieve the file holding the tour (and the decompression utility, if you need it). Be sure to use binary mode to transfer the tour and the utility.

Ftp Problems
If you have trouble with ftp, try these tactics:

- If you have trouble connecting, the site may be too busy with other work. Some sites are *very* busy (with people actually doing work), and it's difficult to connect. Consider the local time *for the remote site*, and try again at an off-peak time.
- The directory listing may scroll off the screen too quickly to read. Solutions vary, depending on your ftp client. Try these commands:
  `dir` *directoryname* `|more`
  If this works, try the Spacebar to go, q to cancel the listing, and `Ctrl+c` to cancel the command.
  `dir "|more"`
  `Ctrl+s` to stop scrolling, `Ctrl+q` to resume

- If you have trouble viewing a file that should be text, make sure to type `ascii` before the `get` command.
- You may need to download the files from your local host computer to your own computer. See chapter 14 for help with this.
- If the files you retrieve are unusable, the problem is usually in the selection of the file mode (ASCII or binary). Many problems can also occur in downloading files to your own computer and decompressing files. See chapter 14 for help with this.

Ftp Command Reference   (page 1 of 2)

Action	Command
Launch ftp and connect to a remote site	`ftp sitename`
Launch ftp	`ftp`
From Command: (or ftp>) prompt:	
Exit ftp	`quit` or `close`
Connect to a remote site	`open sitename`
View a full listing of the current directory	`dir` `ls -l`
View a listing of filenames only	`ls`
View a listing of filenames on fewer lines	`ls -CF`
Select ASCII mode for text file transfer	`ascii`
Select binary mode for file transfer	`binary` or `image`
Change working directory on remote site	`cd directoryname` `cd /dir/subdir/subdir`
Change working directory on local host	`lcd directoryname` `lcd /dir/subdir/subdir`
Transfer a file from the remote computer to the local host	`get filename`

overview / email / newsgroups / mailing lists / telnet / **ftp**

Ftp Command Reference   (page 2 of 2)

Action	Command
Transfer a file, giving the new file a new name	`get` *`filename newfilename`*
Transfer multiple files	`mget` *`filename1 filename2 filename3 ...`* `mget` *`filename`*`*`
Display the help information	`help`

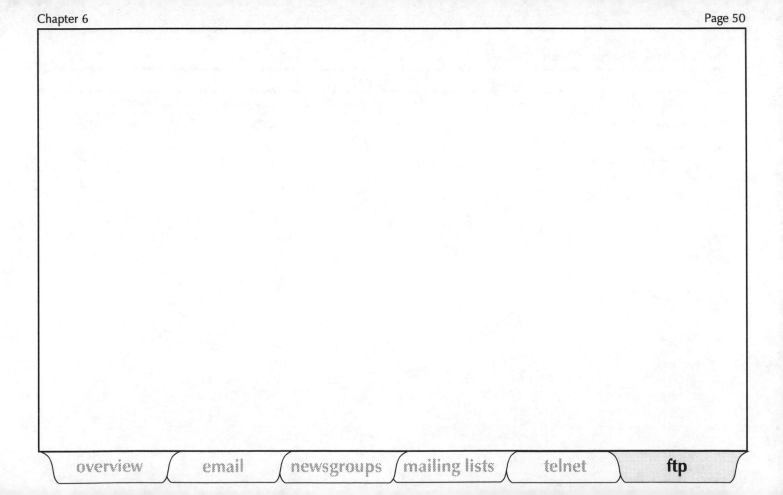

overview   email   newsgroups   mailing lists   telnet   **ftp**

Locating Files Using Archie

Archie's Archives

Using a Local Archie Client Program

Telnetting to a Remote Archie

Contacting Archie by Email

Try This

Archie Problems

Archie Command Reference

Archie's Archives

You have learned to retrieve a file using ftp, but how do you know where to find the file in the first place? Sometimes you see a reference to a file and its location, or someone tells you to get a great file from a particular location. However, if you know the name of a file, but not its location, ask *archie* to find it for you.

Archie knows the location of approximately 2.1 million files available by anonymous ftp, from about 900 Internet sites. The archie database collection program contacts each ftp site once each month and retrieves a complete listing of all available files. Then, the lists are merged into one searchable database. Some archie server sites keep track of all files globally, others limit the files to their own region, country, or continent. It's best to always use the archie server site nearest you.

There are three ways to ask archie for help: using an archie client program on your local host; telnetting to a remote site that has an archie server; or contacting archie by email.

Using a Local Archie Client Program

If you have an archie client program on your local host computer, use it—that's the most convenient way to search. You will receive an answer much more quickly than if you telnet to a remote archie server. Try typing `archie` or `xarchie` to find out if you have an archie client (or ask someone who knows).

Telnetting to a Remote Archie

Most likely, you will need to telnet to a remote archie server. It's easy to do; the only problem is that sites with archie servers receive so many requests, they are often overloaded. Some sites limit the hours they will accept archie logins; others limit the number of connections at any one time.

Archie Server Sites

There are archie server sites all over the world. To be a good Internet citizen, choose a site geographically close to you, at hours that are off-peak. Here is a partial list of sites; you can get a complete list by email. (See "Contacting Archie by Email.")

Server Name	Location
archie.rutgers.edu	New York
archie.sura.net	Maryland
archie.unl.edu	Nebraska
archie.internic.net	New Jersey
archie.mcgill.ca	Canada

archie.au	Australia
archie.funet.fi	Europe (Finland)
archie.doc.ic.ac.uk	United Kingdom

Logging On to an Archie Server

When you telnet to an archie server site, login as `archie`. A few sites also ask for a password; if so, use `archie` for the password.

Choosing the Search Type

Before you begin the search, it's best to select the type of search you want. Your choices are:

exact	You must type the exact name of the file. This is the fastest search method.
sub	Match on any filename that contains your search string, ignoring the case. A search string of `ice` would find matches of `IceHouse`, `malice`, and `MICE`. This is usually your best bet for searching.
subcase	Match on any filename that contains your search string, but the case must also match. A search string of `cats` would not match `Cats` or `CATS`.
regex	Match on a UNIX regular expression. Ignore this one unless you are familiar with UNIX.

To check the current setting for the search type, type:
    show search
To change the setting, type:
    set search *type*   (using one of the search types)

Examples:
    set search sub
or
    set search exact

You can also combine two search types. For example:
    set search exact sub

which tells archie to first do an exact search (which is the fastest). Then, if no match is found, switch to a sub search.

Searching for a File
The command to search for a file is:
    find *filename*
Examples:
    find big.dummy
    find mosaic
Note: Old versions of archie used prog rather than find. You can probably use either command on most versions of archie.

Interpreting the Results
Here is a sample login and a partial listing of the results:

Telnet archie.rutgers.edu
login: **archie**
Last login: Sat Sep 17 14:29:05 from ins.infonet.net
SunOS Release 4.1.3 (TDSERVER-SUN4C) #2: Mon Jul 19 18:37:02 EDT 1993
Bunyip Information Systems, 1993, 1994
'erase' character is '^?'.
archie> **show search**
'search' (type string) has the value 'sub'.
archie> **find unzip**
Search type: sub.
Estimated time for completion: 1 minute, 28 seconds.
working...

Host spot.colorado.edu   (128.138.129.2)
Last updated 06:36 10 Sep 1994

    Location: /pub
      FILE -rw-rw-r—   29378 bytes   00:45 8 Sep 1994
          pkunzip.exe
Host boombox.micro.umn.edu   (134.84.132.2)
Last updated 05:56 8 Sep 1994

    Location: /pub/pc
      FILE -rw-r—r—   29378 bytes   14:11 7 Feb 1994
          pkunzip.exe

```
Host yuma.acns.colostate.edu    (129.82.100.64)
Last updated 22:07  7 Sep 1994

   Location: /software.ibmpc
     FILE  -rw-r—r—   29378 bytes    13:03 26 Jan 1994
           pkunzip.exe
```

This search (for unzip) found many matches, three of which are shown here. Looking at the third match (at the top of this page), you can see that the anonymous ftp site, which has a copy of the file pkunzip.exe, is yuma.acns.colostate.edu. The file is stored in a directory called /software.ibmpc. You can anonymous ftp to the site, change to the correct directory, and get the file (refer to chapter 6 for help with ftp).

Archie displays the matches it found for your search string. If you get too many matches, you may want to narrow your search. And naturally if you get none, you will want to try another variation of the name. You can be sure that if the file is available for anonymous ftp, practically anywhere on the net, archie knows about it. It's up to you to ask the right question.

Refining the Search
You can request the search results sorted by size, by date, by filename, or by hostname (the default is unsorted). You can also define the maximum number

of matches that archie will report, up to 1000 (the default is 100). Archie will allow you to specify which sites you want to search and even which directories to search. To find out how to refine your search, send for the archie manual (called *manpage*); refer to the section on contacting archie by email.

Mailing Back the Results
When you receive a screenful of matches (or a scrolling list of many screensful), you might like archie to send a copy of the results to your email in-basket. Type the mail command, and archie will email the results of the last successful search to your email address. If you want the results mailed to an address other than the one you are using, type mail *name@address* (filling in the actual address to which to send the mail).

Using Whatis
Sometimes you can get additional information about files by using archie's whatis command. The whatis database is a secondary database, which holds filenames and their descriptions (for a limited number of files).The entries in the database are created and maintained manually, rather than automatically. Some

archie   gopher   veronica   www   wais   tools

sites don't bother to create the entries, and some are out of date. But occasionally you can find useful information, since `whatis` searches descriptions as well as filenames.

Type the command

```
whatis filename
```

Example:

```
whatis uuencode
```

Example output:

abe	Enhanced replacement for uuencode/ uudecode
uuencode	Uuencode and uudecode
uumerge.pert	Merge and uudecode split uuencoded files

Signing Off from Archie

When you have finished, the command to end your archie session is:

```
quit
```

Contacting Archie by Email

All of the sites with archie servers are very busy and sometimes extremely slow. You can often get results of an archie search faster by email than by an interactive telnet session—and it frees you to do something else while the search takes place.

To do an email archie search, send an email request holding archie commands to an archie server. Archie does the search and emails the results back to you. Depending on the server you choose and the time of day, you may see the results in your in-basket within a few minutes.

Address your email message to `archie@archie.site` (substitute one of the archie server site addresses). Do not include a subject line. Place archie commands, one per line, in the body of the message. Archie will use your email address, from the mail header, for the return address. (Note: You can direct the response to a different address by including the command `set mailto` *name@address*.)

Here is a sample email message:

```
To:     archie@archie.sura.net
From:   name@address

set search sub
set sortby time
find uuencode
whatis uuencode
manpage
```

Try This

- Check to see if you have a local archie client program: Try typing `archie` and `xarchie` at the command line.
- Telnet to an archie server site and search for a file. For the filename, use a name of your choice, or look for an archiving or compression program. Try pkzip, unzip, uuencode, uudecode.
- Send an email message to an archie server site and send for the Help file, the archie manual, and the names of all archie server sites. In the body of the message include these three lines:
  ```
  help
  manpage
  servers
  ```
- Send an email message to an archie server site to search for a file. Pick something that interests you, and include a `find` command and a `whatis` command for the same search string.

Archie Problems

If you have troubles with archie:

- Usually, any problems with archie are due to overloading. You can try another archie server site or try at a different time of day.
- Interactive session (telnet) very slow: This is due to overloading. Try sending your request by email—it's usually *much* faster.
- Email request not returned: Usually email requests are returned very quickly. If yours isn't, try sending it to another site. Some sites are considerably better than others.

archie / gopher / veronica / www / wais / tools

Archie Command Reference

Action	Command
Run a local archie client	archie or xarchie
Telnet to a remote archie site	telnet *archie@archie.site* login: archie
End archie session	quit
Show current settings	show
See archie's Help screens	help or help topic
Search for a filename (or partial name)	find *filename* or prog *filename*
Email results of last search	mail or mail *name@address*
Search the whatis description database	whatis *filename*
Set the search type to look for substrings	set search sub
Set the sort order	set sortby time set sortby size set sortby filename set sortby hostname
Send a list of archie server sites	servers

archie   gopher   veronica   www   wais   tools

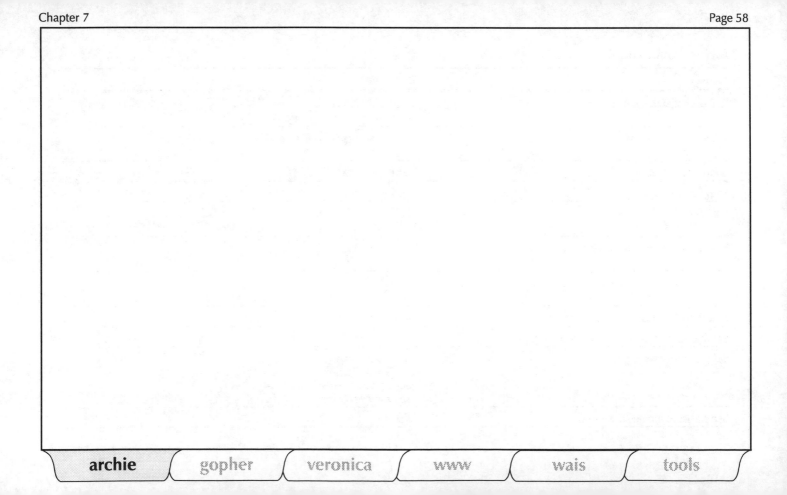

archie   gopher   veronica   www   wais   tools

LOCATING INFORMATION USING GOPHER

Sending Gopher to Find Information

Using a Local Gopher Client Program

Telnetting to a Remote Gopher

Try This

Gopher Problems

Gopher Command Reference

Sending Gopher to Find Information

All that information—how do you find what you want? One of the more helpful tools is gopher, which "goes fer" your request. The Internet gopher was developed at the University of Minnesota (where the mascot is the gopher, incidentally).

If you're tired of all the complicated commands for finding and retrieving information, you will appreciate gopher. The Internet gopher organizes the information available on the Internet into menus. You can choose menu items, which may take you to another level of menu, or a file, or a search, or a telnet session on another computer. You don't have to know the computer system on which the resource resides or the commands to get you there; gopher does it all for you. Most gopher clients also allow you to retrieve files (actually doing the ftp for you).

To use gopher, you must either have a gopher client program on your local host or telnet to a site with a public gopher client. The gopher client you use contacts gopher servers for the menus of choices. Each time you choose an item from a menu, your gopher client automatically issues all the necessary commands to connect you to the site holding the information you requested. And gopher keeps track of where you've been, so you can backtrack and take another path through the menus.

It's easy and fun to use gopher. You can explore all around the Internet, without worrying about the commands. As you find interesting and favorite spots, you can create bookmarks, which allow you to quickly return to a location in the future. Your personal list of bookmarks actually becomes your own private gopher menu, which you can use to visit your best liked places.

Using a Local Gopher Client Program
You will find that most hosts (service providers) have a gopher client program available. Just as with mail and news readers, there is tremendous variety in the programs. There are gopher programs that run on UNIX, VMS, MS-DOS, Windows, XWindows, Macintosh, IBM mainframes, and others. And, as you might expect, the commands vary from one program to another. You may select menu items and commands with a mouse, with cursor movement keys, by typing numbers on the keyboard, or by pressing function keys. The display of the menus on the screen also varies; you may see all text or icons and buttons. But all the various versions just require that you select items from menus.

To begin using gopher, first look around for a menu item or icon. Or, type `gopher` on the command line. Your local gopher will contact a server and present you with a menu. Usually, you can use the cursor-movement keys (up and down) to select an item, and press Enter/Return.

This is the main menu from the University of Minnesota's gopher (the mother of all gophers). You may see this menu or another one to begin. You will be able to get from one menu to another easily.

```
                 Home Gopher server: gopher.tc.umn.edu
 →  1.   Information About Gopher/
     2.   Computer Information/
     3.   Discussion Groups/
     4.   Fun & Games/
     5.   Internet file server (ftp) sites/
     6.   Libraries/
     7.   News/
     8.   Other Gopher and Information Servers/
     9.   Phone Books/
    10.   Search Gopher Titles at the University of
          Minnesota <?>
    11.   Search lots of places at the University of
          Minnesota <?>
    12.   University of Minnesota Campus
          Information/

Press ? for Help, q to Quit                  Page: 1/1
```

Interpreting the Menu Choices

You can tell what each item on a menu represents. Each gopher client displays an indication along with the text of the menu choice. In the preceding gopher menu, notice the characters at the end of each line; a slash (/) indicates the item will display another menu; the question mark (<?>) means that you will be given an opportunity to do a search. You may also see a line ending with a period (.), indicating a text file (document) that you can read. The following gopher menu, from a different gopher client, indicates the type of item with words. If you are lucky, you may even have a graphical gopher, which displays the indication as icons instead of text.

```
          Clearinghouse for Subject-Oriented
             Internet Resource Guide (UMich)
1. About the Clearinghouse (UMich) <menu>
2. Search full texts of these Guides <search>
3. The Internet Resource Discovery Project (UMich) <menu>
4. Helpful Information on using the Internet <menu>
5. All guides <menu>
6. Guides on the Humanities <menu>
7. Guides on the Sciences <menu>
8. Guides on the Social Sciences <menu>
9. Clearinghouse Updates (last updated (9/16? (UMich)
   <document>
```

Navigating the Menus

Some menus are too long for one screen. You'll know there is more by the words Page: 1/2, or more, or some such indication. Depending on your system, you can view the rest of the menu with the > and < keys, the + and - keys, scroll bars, or function keys.

When you have moved down through levels of menus, you can move back up again. The u key works on many gopher clients—read your screen for the method on yours.

Viewing, Saving, Printing, and Mailing Back Files

When you choose a menu item for a text entry, the text will appear on your screen. You can also choose to have the file sent to you (in an automatic ftp), or you can email it to yourself. When you choose a menu item that indicates a binary file, such as a compressed zip or z file, the file is automatically sent to you. Note: To send a file to yourself, you must be using a local client gopher, not a telnet site. The file will appear in the same location as if you had ftp'd it yourself.

If you are using the UNIX text gopher, type s (lowercase) to save a file; gopher will ask you for the name you want to call the file on your system. The command to mail a document is m (lowercase); gopher will prompt you for the email address.

Saving Your Favorite Places as Bookmarks
When you find a good spot in a gopher menu, save it as a bookmark. You can display your bookmark list and go directly to any of the locations. In the UNIX text gopher, type a (lowercase "a") to add the current *item* (file) to the bookmark list; type A (uppercase) to add the current *menu* to the list. To view your bookmark list as a menu, type v (lowercase); or to delete the current bookmark, type d (lowercase).

If you are using a different gopher client, you will likely see an indication on the screen, telling you how to create and view bookmarks.

Selecting a Particular Gopher
If you know the gopher you want to choose, you can type its name on the command line when you launch the program. You will be taken directly to the gopher menu you specify. Type
    gopher *sitename*

Example:
    gopher gopher.crest.org

Signing Off Gopher
When you're finished with your gopher session, type q to quit.

Telnetting to a Remote Gopher
If you don't have a local client gopher program, you can telnet to a public gopher site. You will probably find that the gopher runs quite slowly, due to overload. With a few exceptions, you can do everything on the remote gopher client that you can on a local one. What you cannot do is save or print a file, or save your bookmark list.

Public Gopher Sites
Here is a partial list of public gopher sites to which you can telnet. The list changes periodically, as some hosts become so overloaded they decide to no longer allow public access.

Site	Login
consultant.micro.umn.edu	gopher
sunsite.unc.edu	gopher
gopher.msu.edu	gopher
cat.ohiolink.edu	gopher
infoslug.ucsc.edu	gopher
infopath.ucsd.edu	gopher
gopher.virginia.edu	gwis
gopher.ora.com	gopher
panda.uiowa.edu	gopher

archie   **gopher**   veronica   www   wais   tools

Try This

- Try your local gopher client: Either find a menu choice to launch the program or type `gopher`. Explore the menus, making selections to move down several levels and back up again. Identify menu choices as another level of menu, a text file, a binary file, a search, a telnet session, etc. Find two or three interesting locations and add them to your bookmark list. Then display your bookmark list, and go directly to each of your bookmarks.
- Telnet to a public gopher site and investigate the menus. You should be able to create and use bookmarks, but they will be good for only that session. The remote site will not save your bookmark list when you log off.
- Use gopher to locate a text file that interests you, and email it to yourself. Then, send a file (the same one or a different one) to yourself using a `save` command.
- Use the command line method to go directly to one of these gopher locations. (Type `gopher sitename`.)

Site	What you'll find
gopher.crest.org	state-of-the-art information on the environment, renewable energy, and energy efficiency
is.internic.net	choose `Information Services/Scout Report` for interesting new stuff on the net
envirolink.org	information about nonprofit organizations
cns.cscns.com	choose History, Reference, The CIA World Fact Book, and get info about the country of your choice
info.er.usgs.gov	US Geological Survey
dna.cedb.uwf.edu	biology information
selway.umt.edu 700 (make sure to add the port number 700)	drug & alcohol info, sexuality & AIDS info
gopher.eff.org	social aspects of computer networking–advocacy
asa.ugl.lib.umich.edu	University of Michigan library gopher
wx.atmos.uiuc.edu	weather forecasts

archie · **gopher** · veronica · www · wais · tools

Gopher Problems
If you have problems with gopher:

- You choose an item, and you get a message telling you that it couldn't access the directory, there was nothing selected, or nothing matching: This, and similar, messages usually mean that the site where the information is kept is either too busy right now or down. You may have better luck if you try again later.

- You are unable to do certain functions, such as search for a string in a menu or display the details of an item: Not all gopher clients implement these features.

- You are unable to print a file or save a file: You cannot do these functions from a telnet session, only from a local client program.

- Your bookmarks work fine for one session, but aren't there the next session: Most likely, you are working from a telnet archie, rather than a local client program. Only a local program can save your bookmarks to a file.

Gopher Command Reference

Action	UNIX text gopher command	Your gopher command
Launch gopher	`gopher`	
Telnet to a remote gopher	`telnet sitename` (fill in sitename here)	
Launch gopher, selecting a gopher site	`gopher sitename`	
Move to a menu item	up, down cursor keys, or type line number	
Select a menu item	Press Enter or right arrow	
See next page of menu	> (or +)	
See previous page of menu	< (or -)	
Return to previous menu	u	
Return to main menu	m (from a menu, not an item)	
Search the menu for a string	`/string` (slash and search string)	
Print the item	p	
Save the item	s	
Email the item	m (from the item, not a menu)	
Display details of an item	=	
Quit viewing an item	q (from the item, not a menu)	

archie   **gopher**   veronica   www   wais   tools

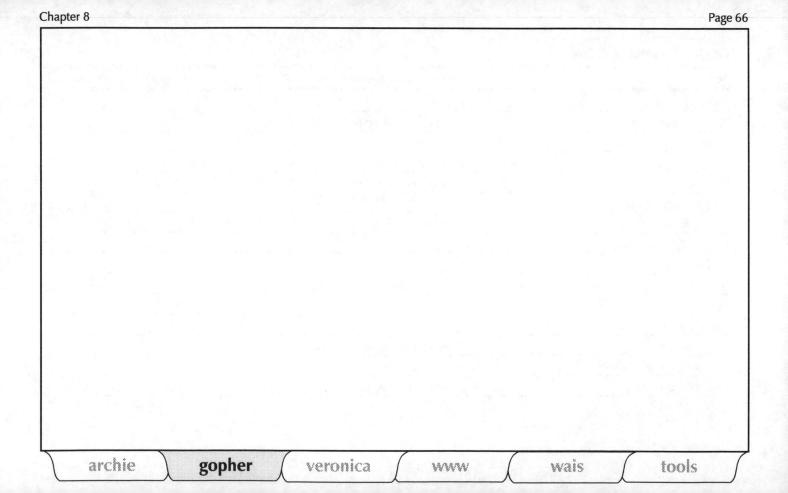

archie **gopher** veronica www wais tools

GETTING HELP FROM VERONICA

Veronica's Archives

Beginning Your Search

Try This

Veronica Problems

Veronica Command Reference

Veronica's Archives

Using gopher's menus is a great way to explore sites and retrieve files, but sometimes it can be frustrating looking for a particular topic. Veronica is the solution to that problem. Actually, veronica does for gopher what archie does for ftp: locate the desired information.

On most gopher menus you will find a choice that allows you to do a veronica search. For example, on the top-level gopher menu from the University of Minnesota (mother of all gophers), you find the option:
`8. Other Gopher and Information Servers/.`
On the next menu, you find the option:
`2. Search titles in Gopherspace using veronica /.`

There are only a few sites that have veronica servers. When you choose to do a veronica search from any gopher menu, you then choose which server to use. Here is the University of Minnesota's veronica search menu. Notice that this is just another gopher menu; you already know how to navigate.

```
             Search titles in Gopherspace using veronica
→ 1.
  2.  About veronica:  Documents, Software, Index-Control Protocol./
  3.  Experimental veronica query interface: chooses server for you!/
  4.  FAQ:  Frequently-Asked Questions about veronica  (1994-07-29)
  5.  Find ONLY DIRECTORIES by Title word(s) (via NYSERNet) <?>
  6.  Find ONLY DIRECTORIES by Title word(s) (via SUNET) <?>
  7.  Find ONLY DIRECTORIES by Title word(s) (via U. of Manitoba) <?>
  8.  Find ONLY DIRECTORIES by Title word(s) (via UNINETT... of Bergen) <?>
  9.  Find ONLY DIRECTORIES by Title word(s) (via University of Koeln.. <?>
  10. Find ONLY DIRECTORIES by Title word(s) (via University of Pisa) <?>
  11. How to Compose Veronica Queries - June 23, 1994
  12. Search GopherSpace by Title word(s) (via NYSERNet) <?>
  13. Search GopherSpace by Title word(s) (via SUNET) <?>
  14. Search GopherSpace by Title word(s) (via U. of Manitoba) <?>
  15. Search GopherSpace by Title word(s) (via UNINETT/U. of Bergen) <?>
  16. Search GopherSpace by Title word(s) (via University of Koeln) <?>
  17. Search GopherSpace by Title word(s) (via University of Pisa) <?>

     Press ? for Help, q to Quit, u to go up a menu       Page: 1/1
```

Beginning Your Search

You will be searching through an index of titles and directories available from gopher menus, all over the world (called GopherSpace). If you are searching for a fairly broad topic, like *medicine,* it's best to search for *directories*. If the topic you are looking for is more specific, such as *aspirin,* search for *title words*. When you find a directory name, you find a menu of related files; when you find a title, you find single filenames matching your search criterion.

Notice the six sites you can search. At the present time, those are the only available veronica servers. All the sites are very busy and may refuse your connection. If one server is too busy, try another one. Also, if you don't find what you're searching for, try another server. The results of a search often vary from site to site, depending on when their indexes were updated.

Notice menu options 2, 4, and 11 on the previous veronica search menu. By choosing one of these options, you can get information about veronica, the FAQ (frequently asked questions) file, and detailed instructions on formulating your query.

Forming a Query

Veronica can search for single words, as well as multiple words. You can tell it to find only certain types of files (such as text, directory, binary, sound, image), specify how many matches to display (maximum), and construct complicated searches using and, or, not, and wildcards. For these specialized queries, consult the file How to Compose Veronica Queries, listed on the veronica search menu.

When you search for a single word, of course veronica looks for all occurrences of that word. If you specify two (or more) words, it finds all titles holding *both* words. If you want to find one word or the other, add or between the words. For example, if you search for windows uuencode, it will find all titles that have those

two words; the words may be in any order or separated by other words. Searching for mac or macintosh would find all titles with either word (a *very* long list). You can also add parentheses; searching for (mac or macintosh) uuencode would find all titles holding *uuencode* and either *mac* or *macintosh*.

A Sample Search
In this search, I was looking for a version of uuencode that would run under Windows:

```
+—Search GopherSpace by Title word(s) (via NYSERNet)—+
|                                                     |
| Words to search for                                 |
|                                                     |
| windows uuencode                                    |
|                                                     |
| Help: ^-    Cancel: ^G                              |
+-----------------------------------------------------+
```

archie / gopher / **veronica** / www / wais / tools

The Result:

```
Search GopherSpace by Title word(s) (via NYSERNet): windows uuencode
→   1. New version of uuencode for Windows
    2. New version of uuencode for Windows
    3. uucode20.zip—multi-part-uuencode-uudecode-for-windows-3.x-    21May..
    4. uucode20.zip 135KB   Uuencode/Uudecode for Windows <PC Bin>
    5. uucode20.zip 135020  Uuencode..ode for Windows <PC Bin>
    6. uucode20.zip 135020  Uuencode..ode for Windows <PC Bin>
    7. uucode20.zip uuencode - uudecode pre windows <Bin>
```

Notice that the result of the search is presented as another gopher menu. The first two items are documents—probably the same document, at two different sites. The filenames ending with zip and identified as <PC Bin> or <Bin> are binary files, holding the actual program. Sometimes you can see different sizes or dates, to indicate a newer or older version. But notice in this case all the zip files have the same name—most likely they are all copies of the same file, stored on different systems. You can choose any one, and the file will be transferred to your local host computer.

Try This

- Find the veronica search item on your gopher menu and choose the option `How to Compose Veronica Queries`. Save this file to your own system, for reference.
- Choose a topic and do a search of directories and a search of filenames. Is there any difference in the result? If you don't find any matches, or the server site you chose doesn't respond, choose another site.
- Find a version of `uuencode` that will run on your computer system.

Veronica Problems

If you have problems with veronica:

- Most problems with veronica are due to overloading of the few veronica servers in the world. You may have to keep trying different server sites, or try at a different time of day.
- If you don't find any matches, try using different words for your query.
- If you get too many matches, try narrowing your search by adding words to the query. You can also limit the number of matches by placing a code after the search string. For example, `-m100` limits the number of matches to 100.

archie / gopher / **veronica** / www / wais / tools

Veronica Command Reference
Veronica runs from a gopher menu and produces another gopher menu. Therefore, veronica commands are the same as gopher commands.

Action	Command
Begin a veronica search	Choose `Search titles in Gopherspace using veronica` from a gopher menu
Quit a veronica search	Choose the backup or quit command from your gopher

archie   gopher   **veronica**   www   wais   tools

NAVIGATING THE
WORLD WIDE WEB (WWW)

Jumping Around the Net Using Hypertext

Addressing Net Resources by URL

Browser Programs

Browsing with a Text Mode Program

Browsing with a Graphical Program

Try This

WWW Browser Problems

WWW Line Mode Browser Command Reference

Browsing with Mosaic

Jumping Around the Net Using Hypertext

Are you ready for a really easy, flexible, and fun way to browse the Internet? Try the newest and fastest growing method—the World Wide Web (WWW, W3, or affectionately—the web). The WWW, originally developed at CERN (the European Particle Physics Laboratory in Switzerland), is based on the concept of hypertext.

Following Hypertext Links
You have probably already used hypertext—maybe without knowing its name. When you can view a document on the screen, see a topic that interests you, and jump to another page or document for more information on the topic, you are following a hypertext link. In fact, since you can now often link to a picture or a sound, the term is properly *hypermedia*.

The WWW is set up as many hypertext pages, with links to many places—documents, menus, databases, graphics, and sounds. When you choose a hypertext link, the WWW client program automatically connects you with the requested information, which may be anywhere on the Internet. Many of the resources available by gopher and ftp are also available through WWW. You can choose which way you prefer to access the same items.

Setting up hypertext documents takes a lot of (human) time, so not all Internet resources have been converted to the WWW format. However, every week there is a long list of newly added resources. Due to the popularity of the web and some of the new client programs for searching (called browsers), an increasingly large percentage of net sites are available by WWW.

Addressing Net Resources by URL

When you browse the web, you can follow the links you see on the screen, from one document to the next; or, if you know the address of a resource, you can jump directly there. Every resource has an address, called its *URL* (for uniform resource locator). An URL may point to a page of text (possibly with links to other documents, menus, graphics, or sounds); or it may lead you directly to a gopher menu, or a file, or a database search. An example URL is `http://www.wired.com/` (to find the Wired magazine).

Browser Programs

There are many WWW client programs, called *browsers*, and more are being developed all the time. The first browsers, which can run on any terminal, are line-mode text browsers. The newer, snazzier programs

have graphical interfaces, can display icons and graphics, and allow point-and-click selection with a mouse.

If you have the "right" kind of hardware and Internet connection, you can install a graphical WWW browser, such as Mosaic or Cello. Other choices include using a text mode browser installed on your local host, and telnetting to a site with a text mode browser.

Using a Local Browser
If you have a local WWW browser program available, by all means use it. A local program not only runs faster and more efficiently than a telnetted version, but it can offer extra features. For example, most browsers offer a "hot list," or "favorite places" option, similar to gopher's bookmarks. When you find a good location, which you think you might like to visit again, just add it to your hot list. This customizes your browser, making it easy to visit the locations you like best. Of course, if you are using a browser at a remote site (by telnet), you cannot save a personal hot list.

Telnetting to a Remote Browser
If you don't have a local WWW browser, you can telnet to a site with a public browser. (Once you have tried

WWW, you will likely want to get your own local browser—talk to your system administrator.) The browsers at these sites each behave a little differently; you may want to try them all and use the one that you like best or the one that behaves best with your system.

Telnet to a public browser: **Login:**

info.cern.ch (Switzerland)	none required
www.njit.edu	www
ukanaix.cc.ukans.edu	www
sunsite.unc.edu	lynx

Browsing with a Text Mode Program

Text mode browsers display hypertext links in different ways. Some show links as bold text or reverse image; others display numbers in square brackets next to the links. Here is a web page with numbers indicating the links. You can select a link by typing the number. Other browsers display hypertext links in bold or reverse image. To select a link, use your arrow keys to move from one link to the next.

```
              The World-Wide Web Virtual Library:
                       Subject Catalogue
           VIRTUAL LIBRARY THE WWW VIRTUAL LIBRARY

    This is a distributed subject catalogue. See
Summary[1], and Index[2]. See also arrangement  by
service type[3] ., and other subject catalogues of
network information[4] .

    Mail to maintainers[5] of the specified subject or
    www-request@info.cern.ch
to add pointers to this list, or if you would like to
contribute to administration of a subject area[6].

    See also how to put your data on the web[7]. *
stands for the quantity of information (under
construction). All items starting with ! are NEW! (or
newly maintained).

    We are looking for icons![8]

    Aeronautics and Aeronautical Engineering[9]
      Separate list *

    Anthropology[10]
      Separate list *

1-96, Back, Up, <RETURN> for more, Quit, or Help:
```

Browsing with a Graphical Program

There are several WWW graphical browsers available, including Mosaic and Cello. The most popular program is Mosaic, which comes in versions for Windows, Macintosh, and XWindows. Mosaic was written at the National Center for Supercomputing Applications (NCSA) at the University of Illinois, Urbana-Champaign. The program is available free, compliments of your federal tax dollars. Note: See the sample Mosaic screen on page 80.

There are also some commercial graphical browsers, some of which use Mosaic as the basis, but add more features.

Try This

- First, find out if you have a local WWW browser program. It's name might be WWW, Mosaic, Lynx, Cello, or something else. If you can't find one, ask someone who knows. If you find one, run it.

- If you are using Mosaic, open the `Navigate` menu and select `NCSA Demo Page`. Explore the hypertext links.

- Try telnetting to two or three of the public WWW browser sites. (See page 75.) The various browsers do not all work exactly the same way. You will find one that works best with your system. Then explore the hypertext links, choosing items of interest to you. Each program provides a command to back up to a previous page (try `b`, or read the bottom line of the screen).

- Each of the WWW client programs provides a way to go directly to another page by typing its URL. Try going directly to some of the URLs listed on the next page.

archie   gopher   veronica   **www**   wais   tools

URL	What you'll find:
`http://www.internic.net/infoguide.html`	a hypertext guide to interesting things available on the web. Choose `Browse the Infoguide`.
`http://www.biotech.washington.edu/WebCrawler/Top25.html` (case sensitive)	top 25 web pages
`http://ug.cs.dal.ca:3400/franklin.html`	a good guide for new users, especially those using UNIX
`http://ug.cs.dal.ca:3400/pub/lib/inet.services.html`	Yanoff's list of Internet services
`http://akebono.stanford.edu/yahoo/`	a great guide to web sites
`http://lcweb.loc.gov/homepage/lchp.html.html`	the Library of Congress home page
`http://www.cs.colorado.edu/home/mcbryan/wwww.html`	the World Wide Web Worm—index to web resources
`http://www.wais.com/wais-dbs/macintosh-tidbits.html`	interesting stuff about Macintosh and the Internet—for Mac users
`http://akebono.stanford.edu/yahoo/`	a great guide to web sites
`http://www.wired.com/`	the Wired magazine
`http://www.commerce.net`	an Internet shopping mall

- Retrieve the WWW FAQ file by ftp from the FAQ archives at `rtfm.mit.edu`.

archie   gopher   veronica   **WWW**   wais   tools

WWW Browser Problems

- Occasionally WWW just freezes up and won't go anywhere. Try the `back` command first. If it isn't listening, and you are in a telnet session, press the telnet escape character (usually Ctrl+\); then type `quit`.
- If you are telnetting, you may have terminal emulation problems. It is sometimes difficult to get all of the pieces of the emulation "puzzle" to speak the same language.

- Sometimes the `ho` (`home`) command won't work. Try the `b` (`back`) command, or the `r` (`recall`) command.
- You may not be able to connect to a link. Just as you found with the other Internet tools, sometimes sites are just too busy to respond (especially during peak hours).

WWW Line-Mode Browser Command Reference

Action	Command	Your Browser Command
Launch the browser	telnet *sitename* (use a site from page 75)	
Exit from the browser	quit	
Go down one page	press Enter	
Go to the previous page	u or up	
Go to the last page	bo or bottom	
Go to the first page	t or top	
Search for a keyword	f *keywords* or find *keywords* (when FIND is on the prompt line)	
Go to a numbered link [n]	type the number and press Enter	
View a list of [n] references	l or list	
Go to previous document	b or back	
Go to the initial document	ho or home	
List the documents you have visited	r or recall	
Display the Help page	h or help	
Display the WWW manual	m or manual	

archie   gopher   veronica   **WWW**   wais   tools

Browsing with Mosaic
This is the Macintosh version of Mosaic. The Windows and XWindows versions are similar.

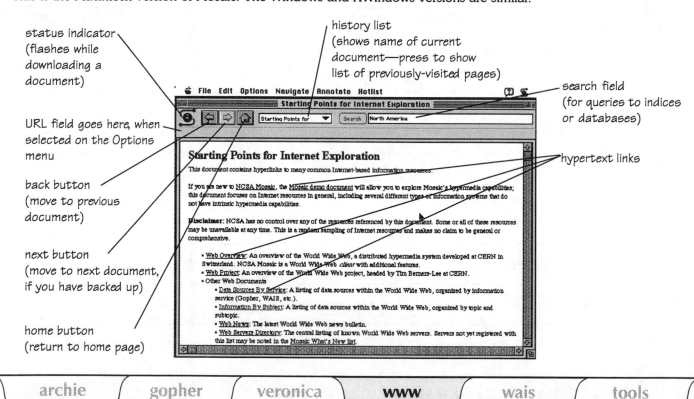

status indicator
(flashes while
downloading a
document)

history list
(shows name of current
document—press to show
list of previously-visited pages)

search field
(for queries to indices
or databases)

URL field goes here, when
selected on the Options
menu

back button
(move to previous
document)

next button
(move to next document,
if you have backed up)

home button
(return to home page)

hypertext links

archie   gopher   veronica   **www**   wais   tools

SEARCHING DATABASES WITH WIDE AREA INFORMATION SERVERS (WAIS)

Finding Indexed Data

Using a Local WAIS Client Program

Telnetting to a Remote WAIS Client Site

Gophering to a WAIS Search

Performing a WAIS Search

Try This

WAIS Problems

WAIS Commands

Finding Indexed Data

When you search with archie, gopher, or veronica, you are searching for *titles* of files available on the Internet. With WAIS (pronounced *ways*), you can search the *contents* of database files. WAIS searches through indexes of topics stored in more than 500 databases.

WAIS (Wide Area Information Servers) is supported by librarians and follows a standard defined by ANSI (American National Standards Institute). The WAIS indexing and retrieval standard can be applied to many things besides text, such as graphic images and sounds.

When you do a WAIS search, you first specify *where* you want it to look (which database or databases). Then you tell it *what* to search for, and WAIS searches the indexes of the database(s) you requested, returning a list of matches.

You can use WAIS in several ways:

- Choose a search option in WWW. This is the easiest way to begin a WAIS search.
- Run a WAIS client installed on your local host. There are WAIS clients available for most operating systems, including UNIX , NeXT, Windows, and Macintosh.

- Telnet to a site with a public WAIS client.
- Run WAIS from a gopher menu option.

Using a Local WAIS Client Program

If you have a WAIS client program installed on your local host (service provider), that's the most efficient way to do a WAIS search. There are many clients available on the net—some text oriented, some with nice graphical user interfaces. If your local host doesn't have a WAIS client, you might try requesting that your system administrator install one (some are available free!).

Telnetting to a Remote WAIS Client Site

You can telnet to a site that allows public login for WAIS searches. However, the WAIS interface is quite difficult to use from telnet—sometimes impossible. Whether you can use WAIS by telnet depends on your terminal type and any terminal emulation software you are running. If you have trouble, try the gopher version instead.

Although the list is subject to change, the following sites allowed WAIS logins as of the publication of this guide. Some sites request that you use your complete address as the password.

WAIS Site	Login
quake.think.com	WAIS
sunsite.unc.edu	WAIS
WAIS.com	WAIS

Gophering to a WAIS Search

If you don't have a local WAIS client, you can perform a WAIS search from a gopher menu. The gopher version of WAIS is easier to use than most of the telnet versions, but is more difficult than a local client. The gopher versions of WAIS have two disadvantages: They allow searching only one database at a time, and they do not provide relevance feedback, which indicates how close a match the search produced.

You can find a menu item for WAIS Based Information on many gopher menus. If yours doesn't have one, gopher to consultant.micro.umn.edu. Choose Other Gopher and Information Servers, and then choose WAIS Based Information.

Performing a WAIS Search

- To do a WAIS search, you first select the database(s) to search (called the *sources*), then do the actual search for your topic. There are hundreds of databases from which to choose. Some WAIS clients allow you to enter search words to help narrow your selection, and some allow you to choose multiple sources before beginning the topic search.

- After you select the sources to search (the database or databases), enter the words for which you want to search. You can enter multiple words, as well as logical operators, such as `and`, `or`, and `not`.

- Depending on the version of WAIS client you are using, you may see a "score" or relevance rating. WAIS ranks the matches it finds, based on how often it finds your search string in a document, the order of the words, and whether your multi-word search string appears in exactly that order. The "best" match always receives a score of 1000; the "worst" match receives a score of 1.

Example search, searching for *computer jargon*:

```
Search->
SWAIS                                    Search Results                           Items: 40
#      Score      Source                           Title                                Lines
001:   [1000]     (directory-of-se)    jargon                                           14
002:   [ 444]     (directory-of-se)    Digital-All                                     167
003:   [ 389]     (directory-of-se)    ANU-CAUT-Academics                               80
004:   [ 389]     (directory-of-se)    ANU-CAUT-Projects                                84
005:   [ 389]     (directory-of-se)    Func-Prog-Abstracts                              23
006:   [ 389]     (directory-of-se)    MacPsych                                         34
007:   [ 389]     (directory-of-se)    NeXT.FAQ                                         86
008:   [ 389]     (directory-of-se)    bibs-zenon-inria-fr                              81
009:   [ 389]     (directory-of-se)    bit.listserv.pacs-l                              42
010:   [ 389]     (directory-of-se)    dynamic-netfind                                  69
011:   [ 389]     (directory-of-se)    eros-data-center                                 94
012:   [ 389]     (directory-of-se)    hst-status                                       67
```

```
013:    [ 389]   (directory-of-se)      internet-mail                    131
014:    [ 389]   (directory-of-se)      journals                          43
015:    [ 389]   (directory-of-se)      prosite                          119
016:    [ 389]   (directory-of-se)      ra-mime-zenon-inria-fr            67
017:    [ 389]   (directory-of-se)      ra-zenon-inria-fr                 59
018:    [ 333]   (directory-of-se)      ANU-Buddhist-Electrn-Rsrces       86

<space> selects, arrows move, w for keywords, s for sources, ? for help
```

In this search, item 001 (jargon) received a score of 1000, showing that it is the best match.

Try This

- Use your local WAIS client to search for a subject. Remember that you must first choose the source (the database or databases) and then enter your search topic.

- Use WWW to perform a WAIS search.

- Retrieve the WAIS FAQ file by ftp from the FAQ archives at rtfm.mit.edu.

WAIS Problems
The problems using WAIS vary depending on the version. The Telnet and gopher versions are very difficult to use, but the concept is great. WAIS clients are getting better and better all the time. If you have problems, the best solution is to install a local client program.

WAIS Commands
The recommended way of using WAIS is to install a local client program, preferably a graphical version. Since the commands for each program vary greatly, they are not included here. Use the Help reference of your program.

USING INTERNET TOOLS

The UNIX Heritage

Finger

Ping

Whois

The UNIX Heritage

The Internet sprang from UNIX roots. When the net pioneers were creating the Internet, they were all using UNIX on their own computers. So, it makes sense that Internet commands closely resemble UNIX commands. Some UNIX utility programs also made it to the net— primarily *finger* and *ping*. Although not all sites on the Internet have implemented these utilities, it's worth trying to find out.

Finger

You can finger your host or finger a user. When you type `finger` (by itself) on the command line, you will see a list of the users currently logged on to your host computer.

You can also type

```
finger userID@siteaddress
```

and find out information about the user. Finger tells you whether or not the person is currently logged on and if he has unread mail. In addition, if the user has prepared a *plan* file and/or a *project* file, finger displays those files for you.

Many Internet users have taken advantage of the finger command to disburse information. When you find lists of Internet resources, often you see the statement "Finger userID@siteaddress for more information."

If you don't have finger available at your site, try the WWW gateway to finger. In your WWW browser, go to URL `http://www.cs.indiana.edu/finger/gateway`.

Examples to try:
- `finger yanoff@csd4.csd.uwm.edu`
  for instructions on how to receive Scott Yanoff's latest Internet Services List.
- `finger copi@oddjob.uchicago.edu`
  for almanac information and important events on this date in history.
- `finger robc@xmission.com`
  for sports scores, standings, and schedules.
- `finger cyndiw@magnus1.com`
  for the trivia of the week.
- `finger coke@ucc.gu.uwa.edu.au`
  for the current status of their vending machines.

- finger for earthquake information:
  Southern California:
  `finger quake@scec2.gps.caltech.edu`
  Northern California:
  `finger quake@andreas.wr.usgs.gov`
  Washington and Oregon:
  `finger quake@geophys.washington.edu`
  Alaska:
  `finger quake@fm.gi.alaska.edu`
  Nevada and California:
  `finger quake@seismo.unr.edu`
  Southern Illinois:
  `finger quake@slueas.slu.edu`
  Utah, Wyoming, Montana:
  `finger quake@eqinfo.seis.utah.edu`

Ping
Another UNIX utility that you may find useful on the Internet is *ping*. Use ping to determine if another host site is online, or to determine if your site is communicating with the rest of the world. It's a good idea to learn the site name (or IP address) of the site nearest you—the one your local host uses to connect

to the Internet. Then, if you suspect that your host is not communicating, ping the nearest site.

The command:

        `ping sitename`

    or

        `ping IPaddress`   (the long number, separated by dots)

Assuming that you can communicate with the remote site, you will receive a continuous display of the number of packets sent and received. Press `Ctrl+c` to stop the display.

Whois

The whois command (an Internet utility) can sometimes tell you about a specific person on the Internet. The names found in the whois database are mostly for individuals responsible for or doing research for the Internet itself.

Try:

        `whois lastname`   (the person you're looking for)

If you're lucky, you may find information about that person.

If you don't have the `whois` command available on your computer, you can send a request via email. Address your message to `mailserv@internic.net`. For the message subject, type the `whois` command; do not include a body to the message. For example, to find a person with the last name of Yanoff, send this message:

```
To: mailserv@internic.net
Subject: whois yanoff
```

When the response arrives, it looks like this:

```
Yanoff, Scott A. (SAY3)
        yanoff@CSD4.CSD.UWM.EDU
    3200 N. Cramer Street
    Milwaukee, WI
    (414) 229-5370

    Record last updated on 27-Apr-92.
* * * End of File * * *
```

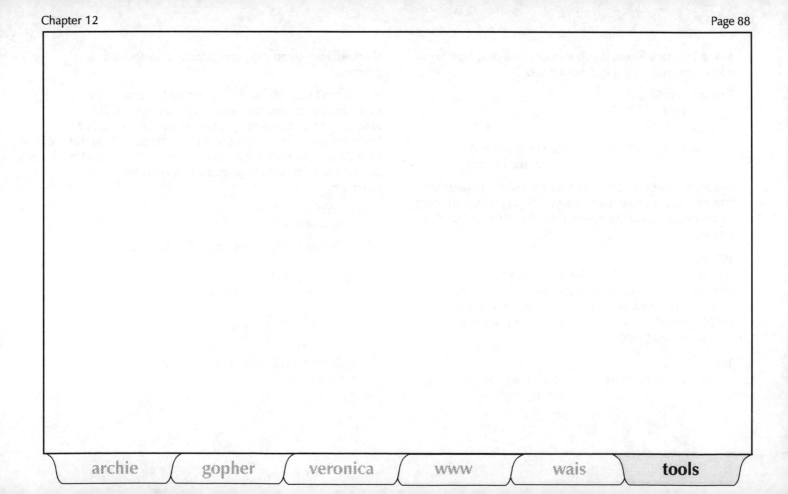

archie   gopher   veronica   www   wais   **tools**

*CHATTING, TALKING,
AND PLAYING GAMES*

Having Fun on the Net

Using Talk

Chatting with IRC

Try This

IRC Command Reference

Playing Games

Having Fun on the Net

There are several things you can do for entertainment on the Internet. With *Chat* (IRC), you can carry on conversations with other people on channels, similar to CB channels. *Talk* allows you to communicate with one other person, so that the two of you are carrying on a live conversation. And there are many games going on at all times—Chess, Go, Othello/Reversi, Scrabble, Shogi, and the famous (and addicting) multiuser dungeon games, which include MUDs, MUSHes, and MOOs.

Using Talk

For a one-on-one, live conversation, you can use the UNIX *talk* program. In order to use talk, it must be installed on your host computer—likely for a UNIX host, possibly on others.

Both parties to the conversation must be logged on for a talk session to occur. One person initiates the session, and the other person accepts or rejects it. For example, let's say that I want to talk with a colleague at `bigschool.edu`. (We have probably pre-arranged this session, or I used finger to determine that my friend is logged on.) I type:

`talk bmoc@bigschool.edu`

If my colleague is logged on, his terminal beeps and a message appears on his screen, asking if he wants to talk with me:

`talk: connection requested by jbradley@ibm.mtsac.edu`

If he wants to talk, he types:

`talk jbradley@ibm.mtsac.edu` and the connection takes place. The screen will split into two halves—what I type goes in the top half, and what my friend types goes in the bottom half. To disconnect, press `Ctrl+c`.

Chatting with IRC

If you want to participate in group conversations, you can use IRC (Internet relay chat). IRC resembles CB conversations, complete with nicknames or "handles," and channels, where people discuss different topics.

You can join a conversation in progress, or begin one of your own.

To use IRC, the program must be installed on your host computer, or you must telnet to another site that has IRC available to the public. If you're not sure whether you have it, try typing `irc` at the command line. If you don't have IRC, check in the newsgroup `alt.irc` for the name of a public telnet site. Public sites come and go, but here are three you can try (login as irc):

```
ircd.demon.co.uk
sci.dixie.edu
irc.tuzvo.sk
```

Beginning an IRC Session
When you type `irc` and begin a session, you first see the MOTD (message of the day). You are in channel 0, a "null" channel. The bottom line of your screen is used for commands, which all begin with a slash. To see the names of the active channels, numbers of current participants, and the channel topics, type `/list` (be prepared for a little delay, the list takes awhile).

Sample list of channels, showing the channel names, numbers of participants, and channel topics:

#cs	15	Friends from Czech and Slovakia are welcome !
#magyar	11	hungarian channel....
#romance	10	say hi to the lovely penguina
#Teen	11	The Teen Channel
#hottub	15	IS THERE ANY TENN PARTY GIFS!
#jeopardy	19	Speed kills on #jeopardy
#hkfans	20	WarmSmile was here!!!!!!! Say "HI" to all!!!!!!!!!
#israel	8	A great channel.
#turks	12	truth needs a soldier!
#friendly	14	%A #Friendly Place In Cyberspace%
#macintosh	14	Enjoy the peace and quiet of #macintosh
#www	10	The World-Wide Web (httpd, html, Mosaic, Lynx, wais)

Type /help for a list of all available commands.

Joining a Channel
You can join a channel by typing the command
    /join #channelname.
Be sure to use the number sign (#) and type out the complete name for the channel. For example, if you want to join the hottub channel (meant to simulate the chatter in a hottub), type
    /join #hottub.

For some channels, you must have an invitation to join. Type the command
    /who #channelname
to see a list of those participating. Then pick a name of a person with "@" next to their name, and send them a message:
    /msg *name* I'd like to join #channelname.

fun   downloading   glossary   index

When you join a channel, you will see messages at the top of the screen, each preceded by the nickname of the person who sent it. Type your messages at the bottom of the screen; they will be sent to all participants in the channel. You also type commands on the bottom line—the difference is that commands begin with a slash.

You can switch to another channel by typing
    /join #channelname
at any time.

Beginning a New Channel
You can begin your own channel if you wish. Type
    /join #channelname
with a new name, which is not on the list; the new channel is automatically created. Then give your new channel a topic, so people will know what your channel's all about:
    /topic #your new topic.

Quitting
You can leave a channel by joining another one or by exiting IRC. When you're finished, use either the /quit or /signoff command.

Try This
- Begin IRC and type /help to see a list of commands. Then type /list to view the list of current channels. You will have to stop the screen from scrolling; the list may be quite long. Then join the channel of your choice.
- Set up a time with friends or classmates, begin a new channel, and conduct a conversation.
- Use anonymous ftp to retrieve the IRC tutorial files: ftp to cs-ftp.bu.edu, change to the /irc/support directory, and mget tutorial.* (three files, called tutorial.1, tutorial.2, and tutorial.3).

IRC Command Reference

Action	Command
begin IRC	irc
exit IRC	/quit /signoff
view Help	/help
list the current channels	/list
join a channel	/join #channelname
change your nickname	/nick newnickname (nine-character maximum)
show the true identity of a nickname	/whois nickname
declare that you are still here but not paying attention for awhile	/away
send a private message	/msg nickname message
invite someone to join your channel	/invite nickname #channelname
create a new channel	/join #newname
change the topic of the channel	/topic newtopic

Playing Games

The easiest way to find out about games is through newsgroups. If you want to know about multiuser dungeon games (MUDs), check one of these groups for announcements: `rec.games.mud.announce`, `rec.games.mud.diku`, or `rec.games.mud.tiny` (for tiny MUDs, like MUSH, MUSE, and MOO). There are also other `rec.games` groups, such as bridge, chess, backgammon, pinball, and video.

Another source of games is through gopher. You can find games listed on many gopher menus, including the mother gopher at the University of Minnesota.

DOWNLOADING, DECOMPRESSING, AND DECODING FILES

Downloading Files

Xmodem

Zmodem

Kermit

Decompressing and Decoding Files

Including a Binary File in an Email Message

Downloading Files

When you get files with ftp, they are stored on your local host computer (your Internet service provider). If you connect to your host by modem, you will need to download the files to your own computer, using a protocol such as Xmodem, Zmodem, or Kermit.

Most communications programs that you run on your personal computer have several different protocols available. Check your program to see what protocols are available; then check your local host. You must use the same protocol on both the sending and receiving computer.

Xmodem

Xmodem is probably the most widely available protocol. To use it, set your personal computer software to Xmodem protocol, and select binary for the transfer mode. Then, begin the transfer at the host end by typing:

```
xmodem sb filename      (for a binary file), or
xmodem st filename      (for a text file).
```

You will then give the command to your communications program to receive the file, and tell it what to call the file.

Zmodem

If you have Zmodem protocol available on both your host and your personal computer, that's usually your best choice. Zmodem is faster than Xmodem, it can send multiple files with one command, and you don't have to tell your communications program the name of the file.

First, set up your communications program to receive Zmodem transfers, then initiate the transfer from the host. Type one of these commands to begin:

> sz *filename* (send a binary file)
> sz -a *filename*(send an ASCII text file)
> sz *.zip   (send all files with .zip extension)

When you begin a Zmodem transfer from the host, just sit back and watch. Your personal computer's communications program will detect the file's arrival, along with its name.

Kermit

Many host computers do not have Xmodem or Zmodem, but do have the Kermit protocol. And you will find Kermit available in most personal computer communications programs. Check your program documentation or Help screens, and find the method for initiating a Kermit transfer. Also, look for the method of choosing text or binary file transfer mode.

When you use ftp to get a file, you initiate a text (ASCII) or binary transfer, depending on the contents of the file. When you download the file to your personal computer, again you must choose text or binary mode. But for the Kermit download, you must select the file type, *at both ends.* That is, on the host, when you begin the transfer, set the file type to binary (for a binary file). And in your communication software on your personal computer, also set the file type to binary. (Of course, if you are transferring a text file, set the type to text on both computers.)

Initiate the transfer on the host computer by typing kermit at the system prompt:

> kermit
> kermit>set file type binary (or text)
> kermit>send *filename*

Wait a few seconds to see what happens. With some communication software, the transfer will begin automatically. Other programs require that you give a command to receive the file. (For example, in ProComm+ you can press the Page Down key to begin the download; on some systems you must type a Kermit `receive` command.)

All done? Then quit Kermit:

`kermit>quit`

Decompressing and Decoding Files

When you find files and transfer them using ftp, you may find the files are compressed. Files which are compressed take less space to store and less time to transfer. You will recognize compressed files by the suffix, or extension, of the filename. Filenames that end in `.arc`, `.z`, `.Z`, `.zip`, `.sit`, `.hqx`, `.gz`, `.zoo` (plus some others) indicate compressed files; filenames that end in `.tar`, `.uu`, or `.uue` indicate special formats that need decoding.

There are dozens of file compression programs in use or that were used in the past. In this guide, we'll cover only the most common file types. You can get a complete list by ftp from `ftp.cso.uiuc.edu` in the `/doc/pcnet/compression` directory (or use a veronica search for `file compression`).

You can find the utility programs that compress and decompress files available by ftp on the Internet. For most of the compression methods, there are programs available for most computers to both compress and decompress. For example, the .gz format is a UNIX format. A person compressing a file on a UNIX system would use the `gzip` program. But there are also `gzip` versions available for the PC, Mac, VMS, and Amiga. So you can ftp the file to your computer (download it, if necessary) and decompress the file, using the correct program for your own computer.

.z or .gz

This is a UNIX format, zipped with the `gzip` program. Decompress the files using the version of `gzip` for your system. You can also request that the file be unzipped before sending by asking for the filename without the `.z` extension. For example, if you want the file called `big.document.z`, you can type the ftp command

`get big.document.z`

for the zipped version, or

`get big.document`

for the unzipped version. (Bear in mind that the unzipped version will likely be 2 or 3 times larger, and take considerably more time to transfer and more disk space to store.)

.Z

These files were compressed with the UNIX `compress` program. The program to decompress them is called `compress` on UNIX, VM/CMS, and Amiga. For a Mac, use `MacCompress3.2A`; on a PC use `u16`, `comprs16`, or `comp430d`.

.zip

`.zip` is a PC format, zipped with the `pkzip` program (or `pkz204g`, indicating the version number). On a PC, unzip the file with `pkunzip.exe` (or `pkunzip4.exe`) or `PC Tools`. You can unzip the file on a Mac with `UnZip1.02c` or `StuffIt Deluxe`. For UNIX or VMS, use `unzip 4.10` or `zip 1.0`.

.hqx

This is a Macintosh format, which converts a Mac binary file into a file consisting of only printable ASCII characters. The conversion program on the Mac is called `BinHex`. You can decode the file on a PC using `xbin 2.3`, on UNIX use `mcvert`, and on VM/CMS use `binhex`.

.arc

This is a PC archival format, which you can decompress with `arc602`, `pkunzip`, or `PC Tools`. On a Mac, use `ArcMac 1.3c`, on UNIX use `arc 5.21`, on VMS use `arcvms`.

.sit

This is a Macintosh format, created with StuffIt or StuffIt Deluxe. You can unstuff it on a PC with `mactopc` or `UnStuffit`. On UNIX or an Amiga use `unsit`.

.sea

This is a self-extracting archive for the Macintosh, created with StuffIt Deluxe. Unstuff it simply by running the program.

.exe

A file with an `.exe` extension could be a self-extracting zipped file for the PC. To unzip the file, just run the program.

.tar

Tar files are UNIX archive files, which usually hold multiple UNIX executable files and/or directory structures. If you are not using UNIX, these files are probably not of use to you.

.uue, .uu, .xx, .xxe

These formats originate on UNIX and are encoded but

not compressed. The reason you might encode a file is that you want to be able to send a binary file via email. Most email programs can handle only printable ASCII characters, and they choke on binary files. (A noted exception is Mime, which *can* handle binary files.) You can use uuencode to encode the file; then, include the encoded file in an email message. The recipient can decode it, using uudecode, and use it as the binary file.

To decode uuencoded files on UNIX, use uuencode or uudecode. On a PC use uuxref20 or uucode for Windows; on a Mac use UMPC Tools 1.5.1, on VM/CMS use arcutil; on VMS use uudecode2. Use veronica or archie to search for the latest versions, and for versions for other computers or operating systems.

When you see a file extension or suffix of .uue or .uu, you know that it was encoded using some version of uuencode. If you see an extension of .xx or .xxe, the file was encoded with a newer program, called xxencode. The xxencode program does the same thing as uuencode, but without some of the problems of uuencode. Decode the files with xxdecode or xxencode on UNIX, with uuxref20 on a PC, and with xxencode on VMS.

Including a Binary File in an Email Message

As discussed in the previous section, most email programs cannot handle binary files, such as executable programs and graphic images. If you want to send such a file by email, you have two choices: (1) Both sender and receiver must be using a mail program that handles Mime, a format which allows inclusion of binary programs, graphics, and sounds; or, (2) Uuencode the file and include it in an email message; the recipient must then uudecode it.

To use the encoding method, first run the uuencode program on your binary file, producing the encoded version. Then, begin an email message addressed to the recipient. You can type a message describing what follows. Then tell your mail program to include the encoded file, which it will append to your message. (The command to include a file varies from one mail program to another; read your program's Help file.)

When you receive an email message that includes a uuencoded file, save the message in a file (see your mail program's Help for how to do this). Then run the uudecode program on the file. (In some cases, you will need to use an editor on the file first, and delete the email header information.) You should then have a usable binary file, just like the original.

If you are using an operating system other than UNIX, the program you use to encode and decode may be called something other than `uuencode`. See the section *.uue, .uu, .xx, .xxe* earlier in this chapter.

GLOSSARY

AFAIK   as far as I know. Abbreviation used in newsgroup postings and email.

anonymous ftp   using the ftp protocol to login to a remote computer for the purpose of transferring files. Login using the ID of *anonymous*. *See chapter 6.*

archie   a method of finding files located on the Internet for anonymous ftp. *See chapter 7.*

ASCII   the code usually used to store text information. Often used to refer to text files.

backbone   the high-speed network that connects the Internet. Formerly performed by the NSF (National Science Foundation) but turned over to private industry in 1994.

baud   the speed that a modem uses for transferring data. Roughly (but not exactly) equivalent to bits-per-second.

bitnet   because it's time network. A separate network of colleges and universities, many of which also have Internet access.

bounce   what email messages do when they cannot be delivered as addressed. "Return to Sender."

browser   a client program used to view WWW documents.

BTA   but then again. Abbreviation used in newsgroup postings and email.

BTW   by the way. Abbreviation used in newsgroup postings and email.

client   a program running on one computer that requests services of another computer (the server). You generally need a client program running on your own computer, or host computer, in order to access resources on the Internet.

Cyberspace   the world of computers and the society that gathers around them, from the fantasy novel *Neuromancer* by William Gibson.

DNS   domain name system. The method used to translate the name of a site into its numeric address.

domain   the suffix of an Internet address, which indicates the type of organization or country of origin. Examples: .edu, com, org, ca, uk.

download copy a file from the host computer to your own computer. *See chapter 14.*

email electronic mail. Used to deliver messages to others at your local site, or anywhere on the Internet, or on other networks with an Internet connection. *See chapter 2.*

F2F face to face. Abbreviation used in newsgroup postings and email.

FAQ frequently asked questions. A file holding a compilation of the questions and their answers.

finger an Internet utility program that can tell you the users currently logged on your local system or information about a user anywhere on the net. *See chapter 12.*

flame nasty attacks against another person.

FOAF friend of a friend. Abbreviation used in newsgroup postings and email.

follow-up a response to a Usenet posting, sent to the newsgroup.

ftp file transfer protocol. The method used to transfer files from one computer to another on the net. *See chapter 6.*

FWIW for what it's worth. Abbreviation used in newsgroup postings and email.

FYI for your information. Abbreviation used in newsgroup postings and email.

GIF graphic interchange format. A format used to store and transfer graphic images.

gopher a method of accessing Internet resources using menus. *See chapter 8.*

host The computer used for your access to the Internet. Usually one (possibly more) computers at a site are connected to the Internet. In an Internet address, the host name appears following the "@." Also called a service provider.

html hypertext markup language. Used to create hypertext documents that can be accessed by WWW.

http hypertext transfer protocol. WWW server protocol.

hypermedia   the extension of hypertext to include links to graphic images, movies, and sounds.

hypertext   text that contains links to other locations, so that a person can jump from topic to topic by following the links.

IMHO   in my humble opinion. Abbreviation used in newsgroup postings and email.

Internet   the world wide network of networks.

IRC   Internet relay chat. Provides CB-like channels for live discussions by multiple users. Can be addictive.

Kermit   a protocol used to transfer files, usually to download from a host to a personal computer.

listserv   software which automates mailing lists.

LOL   laughing out loud. Abbreviation used in newsgroup postings and email.

lurk   a person who reads newsgroup postings without ever saying anything is said to be lurking—or a lurker.

mailing list   a discussion group with similarities to a newsgroup, but all postings are sent to the email mailbox of participants. *See chapter 4.*

majordomo   software which automates mailing lists.

moderated   a newsgroup or mailing list that has a person "in charge," who decides which messages will be posted.

MOTSS   members of the same sex. Identification of gay and lesbian groups.

MUD   multiuser dungeon game, also multiuser dimensions. Very addictive.

net   affectionate name for the Internet.

netiquette   proper etiquette on the Internet.

newbie   a person new to the net. Not necessarily derogatory, unless accompanied by another word, such as "ignorant newbie."

newsgroup   a Usenet discussion group. On other networks, similar groups are called *forums*, *SIGs*, *bulletin boards*, and *conferences*.

ping   a utility program that can contact a remote site and display the route messages take from one site to another.

post   send a message to a Usenet newsgroup.

PPP   point-to-point protocol. A protocol that allows dial-up access to the Internet through a serial link.

prompt   a message sent to indicate that the computer is awaiting a response from you.

protocol   a set of rules or standards that specifies ways to operate to achieve compatibility. There are several protocols available for downloading files from the host to a personal computer. *See chapter 14.*

RFC   request for comment. Official documents that define Internet standards and agreements.

ROTFL   rolling on the floor laughing—your response when something strikes you particularly funny. Abbreviation used in newsgroup postings and email.

ROT13   a method used to code offensive jokes in newsgroups. The postings are easily decoded with most newsreaders, but the coding serves as a warning to people who don't care to be offended.

RTFM   read the f***** manual. Used to flame someone who asks a question that could easily be answered by reading the manual. Usually means *read the fascinating manual.*

server   software that provides a service (such as information) when requested. Server programs respond to client programs, which request the services.

signature   a few lines that are appended to your email messages and newsgroup postings. Signatures may contain a name and email address, pithy quotes, pictures, etc. Signatures longer than 4 or 5 lines are considered in poor taste.

SLIP   serial line Internet protocol. A protocol that allows dial-up access to the Internet through a serial link.

smiley   characters intended to show that you meant a comment humorously. :-)

snail mail   mail sent by way of the post office.

TCP/IP   transmission control protocol/Internet protocol. The method used by the Internet to transfer packets of information around the net.

telnet   a method used to connect to another computer, so that you can login and execute commands as if you were attached locally. *See chapter 5.*

terminal emulation   a method used to make your keyboard act like another type of keyboard, so that your keystrokes are interpreted as the keystrokes from the desired type of keyboard.

UNIX   an operating system that is popular on computers attached to the Internet. The pioneers of the net all used UNIX; therefore, most Internet commands closely resemble UNIX commands.

URL   uniform resource locator. A label given to every resource available on the WWW (World Wide Web), which indicates the type of resource and its location.

Usenet   user network. A network of newsgroups or bulletin boards. The Usenet is not the same thing as the Internet; Usenet news is carried on the Internet, as well as by some other networks. *See chapter 3.*

upload   copy a file from your computer to the host.

veronica   very easy rodent-oriented netwide index to computerized archives. A tool that searches for keywords in gopher menus across the net. *See chapter 9.*

WAIS   Wide Area Information Servers. A method for searching for information from indexed databases on the net. *See chapter 11.*

whois   an Internet utility to find information about users. *See chapter 12.*

WWW   World Wide Web. The newest and increasingly popular method of finding and accessing information on the Internet, using hypertext—and hypermedia. *See chapter 10.*

Index

A

address 6–7
AFAIK 101
anonymous ftp
    40, 46, 51, 101
ANSI 81
arc 97
archie 6, 51–57, 81, 101
    command reference 57
    problems 56
    server 52
    sites 52
ARPA 2–3
ASCII 42, 101

B

backbone 4, 101
baud 101
BBS 18
binhex 98
bitnet 3, 29, 101
bookmark 62
bounce 101
browser 74–79, 101
BTA 101
BTW 101

C

Cello 76
client 4, 31, 39, 51,
    59-60, 101
conference 18, 103
Cyberspace 101

D

decompress 97–99
DNS 101
domain 6, 101
domain name system 101
dotted quad 7
download 95–97, 102

E

earthquake 86
electronic mail. *See* email
email 4, 9–15, 102
    abbreviations 21
    command reference 15
    problems 14
etiquette 8, 13, 20, 103

F

F2F 102
FAQ 8, 20–21, 39, 46,
    69, 78, 84, 102

file
    compressed 44, 97–99
    download 47, 95–97
    plan 85
    project 85
    zipped 44, 97–98
file transfer protocol 5
finger 85–86, 102
    WWW gateway 86
flame 21, 102
FOAF 102
follow-up 102
forum 18, 103
ftp 5, 39–49, 102
    anonymous
        40, 46, 51, 101
    command reference
        48–49
    problems 47
FWIW 102
FYI 102

G

game 94
    MUD 1, 94
GIF 102
gopher 4–5, 59–65,
    67, 81–82, 94, 102
    bookmark 62

command reference 65
    problems 64
    sites 62, 63
gunzip 45
gzip 45, 97

H

host 6, 31, 102
hot list 74
hqx 98
html 102
http 102
hypermedia 73, 103, 105
hypertext 73–74, 103, 105
hytelnet 34, 35

I

IMHO 103
Internet relay chat. *See* IRC
IRC 6, 90, 103
    command reference 93

K

Kermit 95–97, 103

L

Library of Congress 31–32
listserv 25, 28–30, 103
LOL 103

lurk 103
lynx 76

M

mail. *See* email
mailing list 25–30, 103
   command reference 30
   moderated 25, 103
   problems 29
   subscribe 26
   unsubscribe 27–30
majordomo 25, 28–30, 103
Microsoft 46
moderator 18
Mosaic 6, 76, 80
MOTD 90
MOTSS 103
MUD 1, 94, 103

N

NCSA Mosaic 76
net 103
netiquette 8, 13, 103
newbie 8, 18, 103
news 17–24
   follow-up 20
   kill 20
   moderated 18
   reader 19

reply 20
   thread 19
newsgroup 5, 17–24, 103
   moderated 18, 103
NSF 3, 101

P

PC Tools 98
ping 86–87, 104
pkunzip 44, 53, 98
pkzip 98
plan file 85
port number 33
post 104
PPP 104
president 13
project file 85
prompt 104
protocol 104

R

RFC 104
ROT13 104
ROTFL 104
RTFM 104

S

server 4, 31, 51, 59, 101, 104

SIG 18, 103
signature 8, 29, 104
SLIP 104
smiley 13, 104
snail mail 104
StuffIt 45
StuffIt Deluxe 98

T

talk 6, 89–90
tar 98
TCP/IP 3, 105
telnet 5, 31–37, 82, 90, 105
   command reference 37
   port number 33
   problems 35
terminal 32
terminal emulation 105
thread 19

U

uncompress 44, 97–99
unpack 44
UnStuffIt 45, 98
unzip 53, 98
upload 105
URL 74, 77, 105
Usenet 5, 17–24, 105
   abbreviations 21

command reference 23–24
   problems 22
   test 21
user network. *See* Usenet
UUCP 3
uudecode 99–100
uue 98
uuencode 55, 98–99

V

veronica 5–6, 67–72, 81, 105
   command reference 72
   problems 71
   query 69
   server 68
VT100 32

W

W3. *See* WWW
WAIS 6, 81–84, 105
whatis 54
whois 87, 105
Wide Area Information Servers. *See* WAIS
World Wide Web. *See* WWW
WWW 6, 73–79, 81, 84, 105

browser 74
command reference 79
hot list 74
problems 78

X

Xmodem 95

Y

Yanoff 86–87
Yanoff's List 46

Z

zip 98
Zmodem 95-96